Serve gods or be God

Your Choice

Ed Rychkun

www.edrychkun.com
www.miracles-unlimited.net

ISBN 978-0-9810702-9-2

CONTENTS

PREFACE

Life is changing as we know it and so are our beliefs and understandings of what we believe to be true. **Serve gods or Be God** is a powerful expression of the truth and knowledge which is coming forward at an accelerated pace, in this time leading up to December 21, 2012, the end of the Mayan Calendar.

The focus is on us finding God and claiming God within, despite ourselves, our beliefs and the teachings of the world religious leaders. Ed has laid out before you a simple choice with a beautiful metaphor about getting on the Train. Now is the time of choosing, now is the time to take back your power and know the truth. The truth, that God resides within each and every one of us and that we all have access!

This book will change how you see yourself, religion, and the world around you forever!

Mark (P'taah) Sorensen
of the Pleiadian Emissaries of Light
Co-Creator and Protector of New Earth
May 1 2011

FOREWARD

We have arrived! We are perched at the precipice of the greatest show on earth. We asked for it. We said "I can do this!" I am aware that wriggling out from under the deception, the dark and heavy veil of forgetfulness, has been and will be difficult at times—but nonetheless here we are, together in the committed agreement to assist ALL of humanity to release the frequencies of fear, shame, greed, lust (you know—all those lower vibrational frequencies that align us with the necessity of servitude and blind us to the Truth of our Being). In order to accomplish this, it has been inevitable to reveal the darkness so that our eternal light of unconditional love can beam through us and cast the darkness into the light.

The exploration of who and what we are and the relationship with ourselves with God, as God, and/or for god is an exploration well worth the taking. The road that takes us on that exploration is indeed filled with straight-aways that can usher us along at warp speed until; we reach necessary bends that find us face to face with the whys and hows of the sedation of mankind. It is when one finds the courage to stop and face that which has been suppressed, cloaked, and hidden away; to stand up to the deception and simply say 'NO' to any belief or idea that tells us we are anything less than the divine conception of pure source energy; and that within each and every sentient being is the essence of creator; then and only then do we know who we are, the source of our power and finally attain peace.

In the face of misinformation we can choose to be angry with the perpetrators of the lies and delusions but then that choice would align our frequencies and that would be our dominant frequency; or we could simply apply the 'ignorance is bliss' strategy as many have done for millennia. All strategies are but choices. We make choices all along the way. Learning to choose now at this time in the ascension of humanity is made through the heart, not through the head. It is in the yielding to the Divine that the choice is rightly made. We choose to serve the gods of invention and terror or we simply abide in the divinity of our being as the expression of the Divine made flesh.

In the Gospel of Thomas it is written:

(50) Jesus said: "If they say to you: Whence have you come? Tell them: We have come from the light, the place where the light came into being through itself alone. It [stood], and it re-vealed itself in their image. If they say to you: Who are you? Say: We are his sons, and we are the elect of the living Father. If they ask you: What is the sign of your Father in you? Tell them: It is a movement and a rest."

We are the place where Light has come into Being. We are the lives of source creator; of multiplicity and infinite expression. We are pure Love in awe of all creation. What is the sign of the Light in you?

Indeed— it is the time to choose and may your choosing bring you to your highest and greatest expression of the New Earth.

Morganne (An'Ra) Rayne
of the Pleiadian Emissaries of Light
Holder of the frequency of Gaia
Co-Creator of New Earth
May 1, 2011

INTRODUCTION

There is a new Revelation in this book that will take you beyond belief at first.

But if you begin to open your eyes and see what is happening around you world-wide, there is a possibility that may be revealed unto you and wake up a new belief. It is the purpose of this book to awaken you to a new option that stands before you.

Wake up to what?

First of all, the great awakening is that the **Preface** and **Foreword** are written by the Co-Creators of the new Revelation and the Resurrection that is the New Earth.

But really, it is to wake up to a need for each individual human on planet Earth to make a choice.

A choice to what?

It is a choice to first open up to your awareness that there is something not right about how we as a civilization treat each other and our planet and that there is a better choice.

It is because there is something wrong about how the power structure and the monetary system has shifted out of balance to favor the few at the expense of the many.

It is about the amount of joy and happiness that seems to be so evasive, and yet all you really want is to love and be loved.

You sense there is something not right about the proliferation of gods, demi-gods, kings, and queens, dictators, and powerful CEO's, and governments that hold personal motives of deception and greed beneath a face of honesty, integrity, love, and peace.

There is something niggling about the religions of the world that humanity has given its faith and trust to; who have been responsible—in the name of love and God—to create some of the greatest carnage the planet has seen.

There is something not right about this energy.

It is the old energy—Old Earth. It is the way that humanity has simply allowed the high and the mighty to take command of their lives because humanity prefers to serve gods.

What's the other choice?

Well, it is an opportunity that has never ever come forward before. It is a shift to a New Earth that knows no gods because all are equal. And all learn to live in peace and harmony with all that is.

It is a choice to accept the gifts of ascension without meditating on a mountain top for years, without battling life lessons and karma, without paying for masters and gurus, without doing anything but accepting your rightful place of who you are.

It is a time like none other when major changes in consciousness are the prevailing energy—opposite to the Old Earth. It is the new energy—the New Earth— and it has been in the state of shifting since 1987 for anyone paying attention.

It is a time that brings a unique convergence of cosmic forces and a shift to the realization that all humans are actually eternal beings that are part of God. But this is not a God contrived by nor represented by humans. It is not one who is written about in the bibles, and scriptures, in religious books, in tablets, in ancient scrolls. It is not mortal human's attempt to describe their own interpretation of what or who God is. And perhaps many humans have come close to describing God but sorry folks; God has never descended to write anything of or by Himself. Many humans would like to think they are disciples worthy to represent God. There is really nothing to write about because it is all about a mystical, intelligent primordial soup called unconditional love.

So what is this choice and why now?

It is a choice of serving those gods under the Old Earth energy or being what you already are on New Earth. It is a choice of taking back your power that you gave to those gods and their representatives. It is about understanding that you really do have a choice to understand it, believe a new truth, and shift your life's attention to the true love based New Earth.

Why now?

This emergence of New Earth has been escalating for some time now, culminating in planetary forces and a Divine Plan called Ascension. It has to do with the planetary movements and alignments at the end of a 26,000 year cycle that provides a time window to understand the truth of the choice, and to align with it or not. It is a time when enough of humanity has shown they desire a new way.

It is like a one-time Ascension Train that offers free tickets, heading into the new energies of a New Earth. And once you take the ticket, you are accepting a new fate of this new world so you yourself can acclimatize into the new energy—physically, spiritually and mentally. You make a choice to be God.

But the train leaves in October of 2011, never to return again. And it takes you through a chronology of the adventure of transformation through 2012. It is a unique alteration of your and the earth's physics. So if you miss it—and of course you have free choice to get a ticket or not—you are stuck in a much different old energy world.

Yes, stuck. Stuck on the Old Earth.

So why would everybody not simply go through the transformation? It is because it is the individual intent of consciousness and the acceptance of who you are that is the catalyst. It is because of free will that will allow the fundamental belief in yourself—love—to take its course. It is your intent that allows the transformation to go into effect as it is designed to do.

But because you have free will and choice, you can believe this or not. And it is this that your ticket on the train is accepted upon.

So, this book is brought forth to present your choices. It is actually quite simple because for the first time ever in the history of humanity, the forces, and the Divine Plan are opening up to the awareness and powers of who you are. It is happening equally to all. But words and talk can fall upon deaf ears and even if the buzz is prevalent, as it is now, you can still ignore it.

The book will take you to the simple new truth unfolding now in a unique time like no other. Because the dominant religions of the Earth have versions of how the Old Earth transforms into the New Earth, through some form of Genesis, Revelation, Resurrection and Armageddon, it is this that is the attention here. To bring you a new version brought to you during the current Time of Choosing. It precedes a time of Resurrection which is a Time of Transformation.

It is a Time when you choose to board the Train of Ascension to a New Earth where a staggering truth about what we are exists as reality.

Now, be aware that this "truth" is not of science. It is a consensus derived from a knowing of yourself as God,

11

not a learning through intellect controlled by the gods, nor their representatives.

At the end of the day of October 28, 2011, you can take the train ticket or leave it. It's your choice. You can stay and **Serve gods, or be God. Your Choice.**

1

THE RECORD
gods and God

For many thousands of years, mankind has looked for self purpose and identity. What am I? Why am I here? Is there more than this? Is there a God? Humans have quested God and have searched for love and peace—something more than what a mortal life seemed to offer. The quest inevitably leads to finding a God that created us and this place called Earth. Through time, this quest has been entrusted to those who seemingly have found the answers.

This trusting has been the single greatest cause of loss of identity and power that has ever been. It is because these trusted ones, who have presented themselves as gods, or pretended to interpret what God's will and word are, are fakers and deceivers. Why fake? It's because we fake ourselves into believing what they tell us when we already know the answers but won't believe it. The fake is that we let others fake us into their truth. And the fakers who pretend to know the truth, evolve personal motives.

There are many gods

What is god? Notice the little "g"? It seems there are many of them. For thousands and thousands of years it seems it's been a free-for-all for anyone to create some super-human gods or some deity that can do things that they as mere mortal beings could not. In truth, as mortal beings this may be true. But as immortal beings it is not so. Because belief in immortal beings has been relegated to non-human intellect, so has the loss of identity and true power occurred.

These alleged superior gods are in every culture, every civilization—thousands of them! In these myths and stories, particularly the major ones, the common denominator appears to be that these gods all love you except when you piss them off. Whether it is Zeus, Poseidon, Apollo, Mars, the list in all cultures through history is endless. But they all seem to like their indulgences, have likes and dislikes with big egos, and seem to engage with mortals to "taste" the avarice of lower forms. And they like to use their special powers to rule, dominate and create fear. What is common is that the myths disclose how these special powers raise havoc with these mortals when they are displeased.

When they are displeased, then they become vengeful. Religions, cults, spiritual followings and enormous belief systems are formed around these gods. Here those chosen to represent these gods, all allegedly reporting to have such a privilege, compile for lower life not so chosen the secrets to life and the teachings of the gods. And if you are one who doesn't like the belief system taught, then you must watch out that the god does not take vengeance on your folly. And if your belief system is different from someone else's, then apparently you also can be vengeful and take other's lives... after all, it's the way of gods.

The on-line dictionary says **God** is a being conceived as the perfect, omnipotent, omniscient originator and ruler of the universe. This has evolved to be the principal object of faith and worship in monotheistic religions. But **god** is defined as a supernatural being who is worshipped as the controller of some part of the universe or some aspect of life in the world, or is the personification of some force. It seems that God is the Big Boss! And the gods are just in charge of part of the universe.

Well, if you look around this planet there are a lot of Gods and gods who have wreaked the havoc of vengeance. Planet Earth is not a pretty place when you start to look at the recorded statistics. Religion appears to have gained a total grip on humanity. There are 19 major world religions which are subdivided into a total of 270 large religious groups, and many smaller ones. Some 34,000 separate Christian religions can be identified in the world with over half of them as independent churches that have no interest in linking with the big denominations.

Since the Sumerians around 6000 years ago, historians have cataloged over 3700 supernatural beings, of which 2870 can be considered deities. In truth, the possibilities are nearly infinite. It is easy to pick something you can't understand, or pretend to understand, create a point of worship and surround it with a belief. And if you can convince others, pretty soon you have a god and a religion. If you Google this you will find expositions that suggest there are many millions of gods or goddesses.

But hold it! There are those that support one God—the Boss. The major religions of the Christians (Catholic, Protestant and Orthodox) makes up about 2 billion souls. The Islams make up another 1.2 billion souls. The Hindu are a mere 850 million. But now the religion of Chinese with 210 million are on the upswing while the Buddhists account for 230 million. So if anybody wants to tell you that religion and God are not important on this planet, ask them what they smoke. Atheists are at 1.1 billion. Almost 90% of all humanity follows the beliefs of one of these dominant religions. Every one of these has as a privileged monarchy of structure to interpret, convey, and distribute their interpretation of what these gods or God have told them to be the truth.

Does your god or God serve you well?

The question is: Do you serve them? Or do they serve you? Despite the common belief systems that have a face representing love and peace there seems to be a conflict about different ways to attain heaven, show love, have peace, and how to be holy. It shows through the acts of conflict, killing, and vengeance of these gods; for as the gods themselves can take vengeance, so can their followers. Through religious conflict fought over differing ways to worship their gods, and through the quest for power and domination of belief, the century could tally 80 to 170 million souls (the range reflects a lack of precise census).

What has the wrath of gods brought? Although there are many gods who have served others well, there are many more that when you piss them off, it isn't funny according to legends, scriptures and bibles. Some of the more noteworthy are well documented within the good books themselves. Not believing and not listening has a price tag. Here is just a short list; the point being this can be seen in all religions where gods seem to be of the same mind. For those naughty people looking at the Ark of the Lord it was 50,000 that got wiped for their folly. Then god launched a plague for not ending fixed marriage and croaked 24,000 people regardless of who was there. And god delivering the Israelites to slaughter was an act that terminated a mere 500,000 lives. Then 240,000 people of Judah were killed to give god his revenge. Solomon had to appease god with 120,000 lives. And then somehow there were a million people sacrificed for god's chosen people. When god got pissed over premarital sex, only 23,000 had to be terminated to teach the lesson. Then there were naughty Israelites punished for a conflict with David in the amount of

70,000 lives. And when the people questioned Moses, guess who set forth a plague that killed 155,000? The story of Sodom and Gomorrah was about a hotspot for evil that god was not happy about and he terminated everyone regardless of their faith! Everyone! When the Assyrians made fun of god, it took a mere 185,000 souls to be terminated to appease god. When the Tribes abandoned god, 90% of all communities were simply wiped out of existence.

I did not make this up. Check the bibles. And this is the reflection and documentation of the Word of God and the dominant religions. It's about the one supreme God on planet Earth who does not like lowlife sinners to do contrary things. Forgive me folks but even though I may myself piss him off and a lightning bolt may shoot through the clouds at me, this is not my idea of a true God who fundamentally loves all his children equally. And if you are deluded enough to believe otherwise, then dear one, you REALLY need a wakeup call!

So what is God?

What's God? Good question. He is certainly what you believe Him to be. The issue with the one alleged as God is that his alleged laws in religions and cults are written by mortals that claim to know the minds of gods. Has God ever come down and written the Bible? The Gospels? The Testaments? The Acts? The Psalms? The scriptures? Anything? Of course not! There are many that say he has written the Truth *through* them—the God made me do it syndrome—but has He ever represented Himself? Where is it? All the fake copies would not even get into a courtroom. And yet 90% of humanity believe in these documents and beliefs that are *not* written by *any* original God.

There is a big difference reflected in the words religion and spiritual. Religion is a short term physical thing; born-live-die. Follow the doctrine of those who are the interpreters and followers of the gods so they can help you free yourself of mortality. Spiritual is an eternal thing—born-live-die-reborn. You are immortal and eternal and you don't need any middle men to tell you what the doctrine of God is. By accepting mortal teachings over immortal knowing, you so allow dominion of physical over spiritual.

If anybody does tell you what the doctrine is, it's simple to conclude it is a fake religion thing based on someone else's opinion and interpretation. It simply can't be real because God never wrote it. If anybody tries to tell you the doctrine about God, unless they can come up with God's writings, sorry, it's a fake and falls back to the contrived mortal belief about the gods.

So who do you serve? Is it god, or God? And does God really have servants? Does he want vengeance if you don't believe in Him? Is the true God not a God of Love? Are there different kinds of love to get pissed about? Does he truly love you? Does he judge? Does he sell paperbacks on his doctrine? So why do you believe in someone else's God or gods?

Well, the bottom line of all this is you can't see either of these gods or God. It's all an interpretation of what you are taught—which is learning. Or it is an inspiration of what you feel—which is knowing. So how do you feel about this? Do you accept others interpretations and serve the doctrine they create? Either way, it's a doctrine if the source of God or god did not publish it.

So what about these doctrines? Have the people that created them served you well—in the name and deed of love? Or do they take your money so they can fight others about who knows the best way to represent the god or God and impose their best way to love?

Have you taken notes on the news lately; people taking over the dictators? The Vatican harboring secret slush funds? The finding of numerous hidden documents and

18

ancient writings that conflict with the biblical stories? The truth seems to be getting out. But how come now?

Well there is another shift coming on. It's called ascension. It's the thing the Mayans identified as the End Times and the shift in the consciousness of humanity. It appears to reflect a new consciousness orchestrated through some Divine Plan to put an end to what is called separation of man from the real God. It is a shift in consciousness that awakens mankind to the new truth that everything is One, that we are all brothers and sisters, and we have a uniquely built DNA that incorporates a Divine coding of Self very different than what we have been told.

And here is the big one. It is that there seems to be a prevailing current of knowing that we are part of God, an eternal being of light borrowing a body to experience and expand what God is—pure unconditional love. If this is true, no wonder religions don't want you to know this.

It is these End Times that apparently take us to 2012 that is the scene for this, when the cosmic forces, orchestrate as the Divine Plan creates a New Earth—one that has no conflict or hatred. One that has no God or gods to worship or be afraid of. One that is built on peace and love of all things as one.

Sound like a dream? Look around you and see for yourself. It is what quantum science is finding out. This is called the Unity Consciousness. What is it? It is based on the fundamental belief that we are all interconnected as One something, all part of God. It is that the real God is Total Consciousness of love residing within all equally. This knowing has been lost because through the laws of free will and choice, humanity on Earth has always been able to choose dark or light. But dark is a lack of light— evil and dark energies exist where the light of love dims. The unification is that there is no one God to worship for we are all the One God. And inherent within our DNA— those other 10 paired layers that are a mystery, resides

19

the divinity that the majority have simply chosen through time to give up.

Look around you and check this out. It doesn't take long to see in the news that meta-physics and physics are converging through quantum physics. It doesn't take long to realize the magnitude of this consciousness shift. That is the new energy and you are witnessing in the next few years the greatest shift in the history of mankind; and the most incredible progression and lineup of cosmic bodies and forces ever seen. Something is happening.

So now the big question. Are you here to serve the gods, or are you here to be God? Are you ready to understand your hidden, suppressed side or are you happy to retain the status quo? Sorry that last option has new consequences now.

So is this just another dogma? Well, God ain't got a list of books he published because the bottom line is that it's You—all of us. It is for you however to understand there is a choice that you may have never ever considered.

What follows is how you make the shift during the End Times. There is upon humanity now a Time of Choosing. It takes you to October of 2011. Then it's over. You need to understand this time. First I am going to tell you what to expect in this time, then I am going to tell you how you choose and why you need to. The bottom line is that you have to open to the awareness that you are something greater; that you are an eternal being with divinity encoded in your DNA, and that you can create your own life. But you have to get off your old energy of serving the gods and ego, and allow your true self to open through the heart. You cannot bullshit the heart.

You have been used to a certain way of life; learning to think with the intellect, seeing, hearing, speaking, feeling, and acting upon what others tell you is reality. That is the old energy. Now the time has come where you take up the art of knowing; thinking, seeking, speaking, hearing and feeling your emotions with the heart. Therein lies the big difference between serving the gods or being God. How? It's really simple.

That's what a Train Ticket is all about.

The big question is will you also see the light? Will you continue to serve gods or be God? It is your choice.

2

THE BIBLE STORY OF OLD EARTH

The story of Creation

If you can ever read the Old and New Testaments, and the Bibles in any kind of rationality and objectivity, just like you would read any book, you will be truly perplexed about how these stories have so captured the belief and the faith of over half the population of Earth. There are so many interpretations and versions it is very hard to get a picture of what is really "true". But there is a consistency of thought, action and intent in these writings.

The basis for the majority seem to be the Christian writings and bibles that led to proliferation of thousands of species. They bring to humanity a version of the Old Testament where Genesis unfolds a most spectacular story that rivals the best mythological epic. It is about the creation of Old Earth. One of the versions goes something like this:

Once upon a time that no one can define, God is hovering around looking at this dark matter up there somewhere and gets a great notion to create something with his Son. So they decide on the first day to create light. So now there is light of Day and dark for Night. And all was cool. The next day the idea came to shift the water vapor surrounding this matter with atmosphere. That they called the sky and heaven. And it was cool.

On the third day, in their brilliance, they created water as the seas, to let dry land appear and so this was the seas and the earth. But this needed more so they created the grass, plants, seeds, and fruit so these could grow and reproduce. And this was very cool to them.

On the 4th day it was time to distinguish better between night and day so they shone light from the stars and there was the Sun for day and the Moon for night. And that was very cool. But more was needed.

So on the 5th day it was time to create some life; fish in the sea and birds in the air. And they gave them the ability to reproduce. And that was cool. But there was more.

On the 6th day they created special animals like domestic ones, and a whole bundle of beasts. But there was still something missing.

God said to his Son, *"let us create beings who look like us to reflect us so they can rule over all this and care for things".* And so they added a bit of clay and created Adam. But then there was a complication. They could not just create one being of man alone. He needed a companion. So while he was asleep, they slipped in to cut him and take out a rib and then created woman who was Eve. She was complete as she had come from a man. And so they introduced them to each other and all was cool.

Now on the 7th day God looked at what he had created with his Son and they rested, sipping in the essence of its wonder.

But now the plot thickens. God decided that he would create a special garden for these two which would be Eden. It would be their place and would have the Tree of Life and Knowledge of good and evil. There would be a special tree here that would test their loyalty. So God warned them and told them that they must not eat the fruit from this tree for then they would choose evil and would die.

But the evil guy named Satan being the sneaky devil that he is, lurked in the background and he was always trying to upset God's plans. Within the garden was a revered creature a serpent so he suckered him and collaborated with this serpent. One day as Eve came to the tree, the serpent spoke to her about the wondrous powers of the fruit convincing here she would not die. So she took a bite and felt wonderful. Running to Adam to share this, they then realized what they had done. Adam who could not live without her then ate the fruit. Suddenly God was gone in them. They felt shame so they covered their naked bodies with fig leaves.

Well, the next day, God was back and listened to their pleas. But this whining was not enough for God. He blamed the serpent for his folly and Eve for this terrible deed. So he deemed that the serpent would become the lowest form of creature and crawl on the ground forever. He then placed hatred and sin in the heart of Eve so all offspring would carry this. He said childbearing will be painful henceforward because you tried to control your husband you will be subject to him. And you Adam, he said will live life in toil and struggle and when you die you will turn back to dust from where you came. And so Eve would be the One who would break the power of sin and death as all of her descendants would live thus forever.

Now it depends upon which version of Genesis you use as there are thousands of interpretations—usually to suit the group that abide by this word, but nevertheless what

God says is something like this from Genesis: the First Book of Moses:

3:16 *Unto the woman he said, I will greatly multiply thy sorrow and thy conception; in sorrow thou shalt bring forth children; and thy desire shall be to thy husband, and he shall rule over thee.*
3:17 *And unto Adam he said, Because thou hast hearkened unto the voice of thy wife, and hast eaten of the tree, of which I commanded thee, saying, Thou shalt not eat of it: cursed is the ground for thy sake; in sorrow shalt thou eat of it all the days of thy life;*
3:18 *Thorns also and thistles shall it bring forth to thee; and thou shalt eat the herb of the field;*
3:19 *In the sweat of thy face shalt thou eat bread, till thou return unto the ground; for out of it wast thou taken: for dust thou art, and unto dust shalt thou return.*

This is a pretty severe punishment to be taken on by all humanity *forever*. Is this *really* why childbearing is painful and we toil? Is this why we have lost our eternal lives? How much of humanity simply accepts this as their faith and truth? Is this the root of the dominion of male over female? Is this the root of why females are lesser than males? If it is, then wow, what an effective marketing plan! The snakes and women certainly made a big boo boo!

Well knock, knock, hello females, anyone home in that head? Do you really believe this thing about God cursing you forever to be inferior? And knock, knock, hello you big males, anyone home in that head? Do you who are so logical and scientific support this idea of your toil and trouble?

But that is not all. It gets better...

The story of Dominion

If you continue in the Old Testament, assuming you can read it objectively, you get more history on the creations of God. And also is revealed the nature of this God who is quite filled with a need for vengeance when those mortals he created don't listen. As you go through the different parts you consistently realize that this God speaks a great deal to others who he obviously chooses to do his bidding. It's usually those in some place of power and influence, not just the average dude. What comes through is not only the vengeance of the Genesis Book, but time after time, God is telling these so called representatives of his word to get their "stuff" together. He is always talking to them, to Adam, to Noah, to Abram, to Abraham, to Moses, to many... it goes on and on. He is not only telling them what to do like demands about having one God but he makes rules upon rules to follow, like covenants, commandments, acts, and the like. He is telling them how to behave, how to live, how to create sanctuaries and churches, how you pay fees, how to sacrifice animals for payment of sin, how to not sin; he is telling them how to get the rest of the people who are being naughty back in line, or else. And he is obviously lending a helping hand of destruction and power to support the demands.

Some of these lessons are destructive and are real biggies. We listed some before. It is so obvious in the Old Testament as this forms a continuous stream of the "just and loving God" keeping the sinners in line by curses, by death, imposing toil and indiscriminant destruction regardless of who is in the way. Yet, this appears to be simply accepted as a faith of religious reality—by billions. The death, suffering, famine, punishment, thunder, rain, drought, destruction is just fine because of course God *really* loves the people who yield and are servants of the Lord. Here are some examples:

When Cain slew Abel:

4:11 And now art thou cursed from the earth, which hath opened her mouth to receive thy brother's blood from thy hand;

4:12 When thou tillest the ground, it shall not henceforth yield unto thee her strength; a fugitive and a vagabond shalt thou be in the earth.

4:13 And Cain said unto the LORD, My punishment is greater than I can bear.

4:14 Behold, thou hast driven me out this day from the face of the earth; and from thy face shall I be hid; and I shall be a fugitive and a vagabond in the earth; and it shall come to pass, that every one that findeth me shall slay me.

4:15 And the LORD said unto him, Therefore whosoever slayeth Cain, vengeance shall be taken on him sevenfold. And the LORD set a mark upon Cain, lest any finding him should kill him.

And when God saw men were wicked:

6:7 And the LORD said, I will destroy man whom I have created from the face of the earth; both man, and beast, and the creeping thing, and the fowls of the air; for it repenteth me that I have made them.

And when God Sent Abram to a new land:

12:13 And I will bless them that bless thee, and curse him that curseth thee: and in thee shall all families of the earth be blessed

And when the Pharaoh took Abrams wife into residence:

2:17 And the LORD plagued Pharaoh and his house with great plagues because of Sarai Abram's wife.

And so this God becomes quite involved in many affairs of his people and their actions. It has nothing to do with any other people on this Old Earth; it is a certain group he picks on. And when it does not suit this God look out! It seems that Moses is a pretty good fellow with God and God even gives him some very special powers. If you read the Books of Moses, it reads like a Dictator using special powers to set up his kingdom.

In Exodus, Moses hits the road to sort out the Pharaoh because he's a bad fellow and won't let the chosen people go:

7:17 Thus saith the LORD, In this thou shalt know that I am the LORD: behold, I will smite with the rod that is in mine hand upon the waters which are in the river, and they shall be turned to blood.
7:18 And the fish that is in the river shall die, and the river shall stink; and the Egyptians shall loathe to drink of the water of the river.
7:19 And the LORD spake unto Moses, Say unto Aaron, Take thy rod, and stretch out thine hand upon the waters of Egypt, upon their streams, upon their rivers, and upon their ponds, and upon all their pools of water, that they may become blood; and that there may be blood throughout all the land of Egypt, both in vessels of wood, and in vessels of stone.
7:20 And Moses and Aaron did so, as the LORD commanded; and he lifted up the rod, and smote the waters that were in the river, in the sight of Pharaoh, and in the sight of his servants; and all the waters that were in the river were turned to blood.
7:21 And the fish that was in the river died; and the river stank, and the Egyptians could not drink of the water of the river; and there was blood throughout all the land of Egypt.

And so the people were led by Moses but the Pharaoh wasn't having this nonsense:

14:23 And the Egyptians pursued, and went in after them to the midst of the sea, even all Pharaoh's horses, his chariots, and his horsemen.

14:26 And the LORD said unto Moses, Stretch out thine hand over the sea, that the waters may come again upon the Egyptians, upon their chariots, and upon their horsemen.

14:27 And Moses stretched forth his hand over the sea, and the sea returned to his strength when the morning appeared; and the Egyptians fled against it; and the LORD overthrew the Egyptians in the midst of the sea.

14:28 And the waters returned, and covered the chariots, and the horsemen, and all the host of Pharaoh that came into the sea after them; there remained not so much as one of them.

Then it was time for God to dictate the affairs of these chosen people as they headed for their chosen land:

20:24 An altar of earth thou shalt make unto me, and shalt sacrifice thereon thy burnt offerings, and thy peace offerings, thy sheep, and thine oxen: in all places where I record my name I will come unto thee, and I will bless thee.

20:25 And if thou wilt make me an altar of stone, thou shalt not build it of hewn stone: for if thou lift up thy tool upon it, thou hast polluted it.

21:20 And if a man smite his servant, or his maid, with a rod, and he die under his hand; he shall be surely punished.

21:21 Notwithstanding, if he continue a day or two, he shall not be punished: for he is his money.

21:22 If men strive, and hurt a woman with child, so that her fruit depart from her, and yet no mischief follow: he shall be surely punished, according as the woman's husband will lay upon him; and he shall pay as the judges determine.

21:23 And if any mischief follow, then thou shalt give life for life,

21:24 Eye for eye, tooth for tooth, hand for hand, foot for foot,

21:25 Burning for burning, wound for wound, stripe for stripe.

21:26 And if a man smite the eye of his servant, or the eye of his maid, that it perish; he shall let him go free for his eye's sake.

21:27 And if he smite out his manservant's tooth, or his maidservant's tooth; he shall let him go free for his tooth's sake.

And tell about special robes for the "anointed" ones:

28:1 And take thou unto thee Aaron thy brother, and his sons with him, from among the children of Israel, that he may minister unto me in the priest's office, even Aaron, Nadab and Abihu, Eleazar and Ithamar, Aaron's sons.

28:2 And thou shalt make holy garments for Aaron thy brother for glory and for beauty.

28:3 And thou shalt speak unto all that are wise hearted, whom I have filled with the spirit of wisdom, that they may make Aaron's garments to consecrate him, that he may minister unto me in the priest's office.

28:4 And these are the garments which they shall make; a breastplate, and an ephod, and a robe, and a broidered coat, a mitre, and a girdle: and they shall make holy garments for Aaron thy brother, and his sons, that he may minister unto me in the priest's office.

28:5 And they shall take gold, and blue, and purple, and scarlet, and fine linen.

28:6 And they shall make the ephod of gold, of blue, and of purple, of scarlet, and fine twined linen, with cunning work.

This is all to set up the holy sanctuary (churches) for these chosen ones, and even set some rules for contributions like taxes:

30:11 And the LORD spake unto Moses, saying,
30:12 When thou takest the sum of the children of Israel after their number, then shall they give every man a ransom for his soul unto the LORD, when thou numberest them; that there be no plague among them, when thou numberest them.
30:13 This they shall give, every one that passeth among them that are numbered, half a shekel after the shekel of the sanctuary: (a shekel is twenty gerahs:) an half shekel shall be the offering of the LORD.
30:14 Every one that passeth among them that are numbered, from twenty years old and above, shall give an offering unto the LORD.
30:15 The rich shall not give more, and the poor shall not give less than half a shekel, when they give an offering unto the LORD, to make an atonement for your souls.
30:16 And thou shalt take the atonement money of the children of Israel, and shalt appoint it for the service of the tabernacle of the congregation; that it may be a memorial unto the children of Israel before the LORD, to make an atonement for your souls.

The Book of Leviticus is all about setting up the priest hood and ensuring that offerings are made to God as acknowledgement of their sins:

1:1 And the LORD called unto Moses, and spake unto him out of the tabernacle of the congregation, saying,
1:2 Speak unto the children of Israel, and say unto them, If any man of you bring an offering unto the LORD, ye shall bring your offering of the cattle, even of the herd, and of the flock.

1:3 If his offering be a burnt sacrifice of the herd, let him offer a male without blemish: he shall offer it of his own voluntary will at the door of the tabernacle of the congregation before the LORD.

1:4 And he shall put his hand upon the head of the burnt offering; and it shall be accepted for him to make atonement for him.

1:5 And he shall kill the bullock before the LORD: and the priests, Aaron's sons, shall bring the blood, and sprinkle the blood round about upon the altar that is by the door of the tabernacle of the congregation.

1:6 And he shall flay the burnt offering, and cut it into his pieces.

1:7 And the sons of Aaron the priest shall put fire upon the altar, and lay the wood in order upon the fire:

And then he set up the administrative power for priests and the pricing policy for redemption:

27:1   And the LORD spake unto Moses, saying,

27:2   Speak unto the children of Israel, and say unto them, When a man shall make a singular vow, the persons shall be for the LORD by thy estimation.

27:3   And thy estimation shall be of the male from twenty years old even unto sixty years old, even thy estimation shall be fifty shekels of silver, after the shekel of the sanctuary.

27:4   And if it be a female, then thy estimation shall be thirty shekels.

27:5   And if it be from five years old even unto twenty years old, then thy estimation shall be of the male twenty shekels, and for the female ten shekels.

27:6   And if it be from a month old even unto five years old, then thy estimation shall be of the male five shekels of silver, and for the female thy estimation shall be three shekels of silver.

27:7   And if it be from sixty years old and above; if it be a male, then thy estimation shall be fifteen shekels, and for the female ten shekels.

27:8   But if he be poorer than thy estimation, then he shall present himself before the priest, and the priest shall value him; according to his ability that vowed shall the priest value him.

27:9   And if it be a beast, whereof men bring an offering unto the LORD, all that any man giveth of such unto the LORD shall be holy.

27:10 He shall not alter it, nor change it, a good for a bad, or a bad for a good: and if he shall at all change beast for beast, then it and the exchange thereof shall be holy.

27:11 And if it be any unclean beast, of which they do not offer a sacrifice unto the LORD, then he shall present the beast before the priest:

27:12 And the priest shall value it, whether it be good or bad: as thou valuest it, who art the priest, so shall it be.

27:13 But if he will at all redeem it, then he shall add a fifth part thereof unto thy estimation.

27:14 And when a man shall sanctify his house to be holy unto the LORD, then the priest shall estimate it, whether it be good or bad: as the priest shall estimate it, so shall it stand.

27:15 And if he that sanctified it will redeem his house, then he shall add the fifth part of the money of thy estimation unto it, and it shall be his.

27:16 And if a man shall sanctify unto the LORD some part of a field of his possession, then thy estimation shall be according to the seed thereof: an homer of barley seed shall be valued at fifty shekels of silver.

27:17 If he sanctify his field from the year of jubilee, according to thy estimation it shall stand.

27:18 But if he sanctify his field after the jubilee, then the priest shall reckon unto him the money according to *the years that remain, even unto the year of the jubilee, and it shall be abated from thy estimation.*

27:19 And if he that sanctified the field will in any wise redeem it, then he shall add the fifth part of the money of thy estimation unto it, and it shall be assured to him.

27:20 And if he will not redeem the field, or if he have sold the field to another man, it shall not be redeemed any more.

27:21 But the field, when it goeth out in the jubilee, shall be holy unto the LORD, as a field devoted; the possession thereof shall be the priest's.

27:22 And if a man sanctify unto the LORD a field which he hath bought, which is not of the fields of his possession;

27:23 Then the priest shall reckon unto him the worth of thy estimation, even unto the year of the jubilee: and he shall give thine estimation in that day, as a holy thing unto the LORD.

27:24 In the year of the jubilee the field shall return unto him of whom it was bought, even to him to whom the possession of the land did belong.

27:25 And all thy estimations shall be according to the shekel of the sanctuary: twenty gerahs shall be the shekel.

27:26 Only the firstling of the beasts, which should be the LORD'S firstling, no man shall sanctify it; whether it be ox, or sheep: it is the LORD'S.

27:27 And if it be of an unclean beast, then he shall redeem it according to thine estimation, and shall add a fifth part of it thereto: or if it be not redeemed, then it shall be sold according to thy estimation.

When you get to the Book of Numbers, it's all about a census counting the people to see who is fit for military duty. This God is preparing for war. And they are to serve God and sanctuary:

1:1 And the LORD spake unto Moses in the wilderness of Sinai, in the tabernacle of the congregation, on the first day of the second month, in the second year after they were come out of the land of Egypt, saying,

1:2 Take ye the sum of all the congregation of the children of Israel, after their families, by the house of their fathers, with the number of their names, every male by their polls;

1:3 From twenty years old and upward, all that are able to go forth to war in Israel: thou and Aaron shall number them by their armies.

To serve who?

3:5 And the LORD spake unto Moses, saying,

3:6 Bring the tribe of Levi near, and present them before Aaron the priest, that they may minister unto him.

3:7 And they shall keep his charge, and the charge of the whole congregation before the tabernacle of the congregation, to do the service of the tabernacle.

And there is a price for sin:

5:5 And the LORD spake unto Moses, saying,

5:6 Speak unto the children of Israel, When a man or woman shall commit any sin that men commit, to do a trespass against the LORD, and that person be guilty;

5:7 Then they shall confess their sin which they have done: and he shall recompense his trespass with the principal thereof, and add unto it the fifth part thereof, and give it unto him against whom he hath trespassed.

5:8 But if the man have no kinsman to recompense the trespass unto, let the trespass be recompensed unto the LORD, even to the priest; beside the ram of the atonement, whereby an atonement shall be made for him.

And more for not obeying:

*14:26 And the LORD spake unto Moses and unto Aaron,
saying,*
*14:27 How long shall I bear with this evil congregation,
which murmur against me? I have heard the
murmurings of the children of Israel, which they murmur
against me.*
*14:28 Say unto them, As truly as I live, saith the LORD,
as ye have spoken in mine ears, so will I do to you:*
*14:29 Your carcases shall fall in this wilderness; and all
that were numbered of you, according to your whole
number, from twenty years old and upward, which have
murmured against me,*
*14:30 Doubtless ye shall not come into the land,
concerning which I sware to make you dwell therein,
save Caleb the son of Jephunneh, and Joshua the son of
Nun.*
*14:31 But your little ones, which ye said should be a
prey, them will I bring in, and they shall know the land
which ye have despised.*
*14:32 But as for you, your carcases, they shall fall in
this wilderness.*
*14:33 And your children shall wander in the wilderness
forty years, and bear your whoredoms, until your
carcases be wasted in the wilderness.*

The Book of Deuteronomy is about creating regulations:

*4:35 Unto thee it was showed, that thou mightest know
that the LORD he is God; there is none else beside him.*
*4:39 Know therefore this day, and consider it in thine
heart, that the LORD he is God in heaven above, and
upon the earth beneath: there is none else.*
*4:40 Thou shalt keep therefore his statutes, and his
commandments, which I command thee this day, that it
may go well with thee, and with thy children after thee,*

and that thou mayest prolong thy days upon the earth,
which the LORD thy God giveth thee, for ever.
4:45   These are the testimonies, and the statutes, and
the judgments, which Moses spake unto the children of
Israel, after they came forth out of Egypt,
4:1   Now therefore hearken, O Israel, unto the statutes
and unto the judgments, which I teach you, for to do
them, that ye may live, and go in and possess the land
which the LORD God of your fathers giveth you.
4:2   Ye shall not add unto the word which I command
you, neither shall ye diminish ought from it, that ye may
keep the commandments of the LORD your God which I
command you.

As the bible story progresses, God even has a say in rules and regulations that are almost like reading a current day set of Acts and Statutes, or like the regulations of the IRS. He even has a hand at commerce to fine those that disobey, or do not follow the rules he has conveyed. He even takes a piece of the action in gold! But you just can't mail it to him or take a sky bus up to deliver it, you have to give all or part of it to guess who? Yes, the Church, the Priests!

This God is pretty set in his ways of reigning upon his creation of Old Earth with Dominion and Vengeance? It is very difficult to escape this undeniable aspect of this mythology.

As you continue through the various books of the bible you see how a group of wise men knowing in the skills of dominion set up the infrastructure of the Church to overlord and dominate. It is all done through the word of God as interpreted by men.

The Book of Isaiah, sets the prophesies of death and destruction for the nations in 17:1 Syrian and Israel. See 18:6 for Ethiopia, 19:1 for Egypt, 21:1 for Babylon, 21:11 for Edon, 21:13 for Arabia, 22:1 for Jeruselum,

23:1 for Tyre and even 24:1 for Planet Earth. No one messes with this god.

The Book of Deuteronomy is basically the administrative laws that deal with False Prophets 13:1. Tithing is 14:22, Debts 15:1, and the punishment-reward policing system by the high priests as Blessing in 28:3 and Curses in 28:15.

The interesting aspect of this is that in addition to this being the "truth" for Christianity, it also is the basis for the "truth" of the Islam when Mohammed, centuries later, brought this story to his people to create the Islam religion of the Koran. This brings the toll up to about 4.3 billion people that believe this as a foundation for humanity.

The story of Christ

And then, as you head into the New Testament and the Gospels, there is this incredible story of Christ. The worst place to look for continuity or agreement on this is the Gospels of Mark, Matthew, Luke, and John that are the definitive "truth". As an aside, this topic has surfaced with great gusto in the current consciousness, and many many credible researchers, historians and authors have come up with a totally different picture. Check out the books *Magdalene Legacy* by Lawrence Gardener or the *Holy Blood and the Holy Grail*. See them make a total mockery of the gospels.

In any case the New Testament part about Christ goes something like this.

One day Mary became pregnant and had a baby by virgin birth. It happened in a manger on 25th of December. The funny part here is that no one can even peg the right year of birth, never mind the month and day. Anyway, because of a potential threat to the ruler, the kid named Jesus had to be taken away to be hidden in Egypt.

Some time later, when he is around 30 years old he comes back to begin a ministry and because he seems to have these great healing abilities, plus he is able to raise some dead guys, he gets some popularity and builds a group of followers, his disciples. There are many that he heals and he preaches his word. And being a humble fellow, he is careful of not portraying himself as having a relationship with God that would piss anybody off, like the priests by saying he is the Messiah come to save people. Of course the people call him Messiah, Lord and Son of God.

Well, one day, as his following had grown and he was becoming quite a sensation in his healings, he decided to heal someone on the Sabbath—a big no, no. So that pissed off a big group and his following was divided. By this time people were saying he was the Messiah and the Son of God because he had these powers. Of course the Priests were not at all happy about this, nor was the ruler of the time, Pilates.

The next big issue came when he allowed an alleged whore who he had forgiven—Mary Magdalene—to be present to worship him within the meeting of his disciples. One, Judas, reacted to this so Jesus countered it in a way that pissed Judas off. Judas was a pretty rotten fellow anyway so this little episode set the scene for the betrayal of Jesus and the mob violence.

And so Jesus and a few were arrested and tried. But Pilates could not find an issue to punish him on. But the people, the army and the priests had different ideas and took it upon themselves to execute him through the crucifixion. And so they hauled him and two others to the hill and raised them on the crosses to die.

After the death, he was placed in a tomb from which he disappeared. Three days later, he appears again and visits his old buddies to forgive them. Then he ascends into the heavens.

39

Well of course all shook in fear because they just witnessed the ascension of the Son of God. And then there was the realization that this fellow named Jesus Christ was the Son of God and did come to save humanity from their sins.

And it is here that the whole bible system comes back to the beginning of creation and Eve's responsibility. Everything in it is to build a faith that Jesus Christ is the Messiah, the Son of a living God. If you believe this you will have eternal life because of what he has done for you.

Now, if you care to check into the research here and the new documents that have surfaced, it seems that our dear Jesus headed for Mystery schools in Egypt and a lot of places to learn all about the esoteric arts. And so he taught and illustrated these arts. Both his Mother and Father were skilled in this. And he did not really die on the cross, and he lived to a ripe old age, after marrying Mary Magdalene and having several children. Interestingly enough, these "arts" that he taught, appear to ones that this New Earth, and this whole thing about ascension through the Ed Times, is all about.

This is a pretty enormous divergence from the biblical myth. It all rings of a contrived story that already knew some history and could select the parts they wanted to conform to their objectives. Of course the bible was not written until hundreds of years later so they had a pretty good base to create their purpose and write the new myth from.

Also, the big argument here between Islam and Christian and Jewish faith is related to opinions about Christ. Islamic maintains that Christ was a prophet, not a Son of God... and so the story churns... Yet for 1500 years, this story has dominated the consciousness of humanity, regardless of versions or consistency, regardless of any scientific discrepancies.

Who is the true God?

Whichever way you choose to try to paint this picture, it cannot be anything but another "god" who threatens, curses, kills indiscriminately, imposes judgments, is jealous, and protective of his ego. He demands obedience and clearly issues warnings that he is the almighty powerful god demanding servitude. He uses his powers to maintain dominance. Interestingly enough, he chooses a chronology of representatives who he "speaks to, and through" not in other places on his Old Earth, but only with one place and with his "chosen people" that he himself persecutes, maims, kills and reaps destruction upon, keeping in fear and toil. Yet he rewards the "righteous" who serve his bidding. And worst of all, this god has no place for women as they are the root of evil and sin.

If you can read through this epic saga for what it presents over and over, it is a picture of a mad ruler with special powers over life and death that sets up his kingdom. First he must conquer his followers by fear. Then he sets up the administrative, commercial, sociological, moral and ethic regulations. He imposes acts and statutes and then a police force of religious chosen ones, plus ways to police, control and collect dues. Of course the method of collecting revenues is vital to this kingdom. He builds his power to maintain and execute dominion, go to war, and protect the kingdom. It is a place that his chosen ones allow a dogmatic deliverance for the ego of those ruling. Why? Because they represent a just god of love who has just commandments which he is willing to waive and launch death and destruction if they do not behave. But if they do behave, the chosen ones can give these poor sinful, souls ridden with sin a break—if and only if they behold, worship and serve.

This particular model is one that the Vatican has held to, and it is a model that has proliferated within nations and

41

within major corporations. It makes humans a commercial product. In truth this is a commercial, moral and military model that has been in place for centuries, built specifically for the indulgence and dominion of the few. And who was it that set it up? God—or perhaps just mouthpieces for god?

And although there is wisdom in the Psalms and some of the writings, it is effectively lip service from a god who does not engage in this himself, nor do his chosen ones, particularly in support and practice. For they also kill and destroy indiscriminately those who are deemed sinners and non-believers. The most grueling record of this was the Inquisition. Yet there is no doubt there are pieces of wisdom as part of this epic story that conveys the half truths. It is what believers cling to, support and preach, completely overlooking the explicit fact within the vast majority of these writings that they serve a contrived god's will. The only conclusion one can really make is that something is amiss here and those billions of followers are really believing in another god created by man, not the true God.

The Christ Consciousness

When you finally get to the end, to the final Book of Revelation, when the ascended Christ comes back, the story is presented to impose an automatic policing system of threat and destruction for mankind. And it is Christ, the Son of God—the one that helped Dad create the Old Earth that bears the warning about the End Times. It is that Satan will be crushed (20:7) and there will be a final Judgment day (20:11), there will be a new heaven on Earth (21:1) where a new Jerusalem will rise (21:9) and when he comes it will be swift to judge if you are not in the accounting ledger (22:7) that is within the Time of the End (22:10). It is this threat that polices the believers and is the major theme in the vast writings.

42

The other aspect that vibrates with much of humanity has to do with this man called Christ who came down to prophesize the Revelation of End Time. The story, part contrived, part truth reflects a consciousness of love and peace, despite the conclusion that it is written with a possible contrived mortal purpose of a manifesto of dominion. It draws out a theme that this Christ, who was deemed a Prophet or the Son of God later, reflected a consciousness so many people quietly and inherently would like to believe in—a New Earth of peace and love.

It is this aspect of the stories, despite the motivations of their creation, that in all due regards to the biblical system, has kept this Christ spark alive in the story of Christ or Allah, or whatever. And regardless of whether he was deemed as a prophet, Messiah, Son of God or whatever, the legend carries an underlying energy of something that is wanton in all—like an encoding within the essence of humanity; their DNA.

Even though the four gospels upon which the New Testament was based on were written between 75 and 100 years after Christ, by unknown authors, and are conflictive in their stories, in essence, it seems that Christ was indeed a very unusual fellow. Not only was he capable of creating some very unusual miracles, he was responsible for showing a new way of thought—that of being aligned with the real God of truth and love, and we all are Sons and Daughters of God. It is this that is surfacing in these times. And for what it is worth, he is responsible for a consciousness, a way of thinking and living that is parallel to this revolution of thought surfacing during these current End Times.

It is about the Christ Consciousness. The human mind has spiritual currents running through its thought streams. These streams contain vital information from

43

Spirit that is highly valuable to humans. Spirit is the source of everything TRUE, BEAUTIFUL, and GOOD and conveys these ideals through the human mind that intersect with a person's beliefs, helping the individual ascend into the higher information that uplifts and improves the quality of life.

In human life, spiritual growth is achieved by aligning with these spiritual currents that come from both the personality and mind of Spirit by intellectual assent and emotional devotion. Christ Consciousness is the growing human recognition and blending of the human evolutionary (or ego) mind with the Divine Mind and the Divine Personality that is the source of human happiness and fulfillment. This awareness accrues over time within the consciousness of human thinking when intention, attention, and openness is focused on knowing who and what is that "christed" state of being—that higher mindedness of enlightenment.

As this awareness in the human mind grows and strengthens, life becomes more liberated, joyful, peaceful, and love-dominated. The fear which creates isolation and despair begins to diminish in thought and feeling. You are free to live the life you were born to live —as a child of Spirit in a love-filled and supportive universe.

The highest state of intellectual development and emotional maturity is sometimes termed the "christed" state because of the sacredness and purity of the individual who has achieved it. Jesus achieved this in his human life, and was given this term before his name as the recognition of his achievement of this spiritual status. This path is open to anyone regardless of their religious tradition if and when he or she is open to become a living vessel of LOVE and TRUTH on the planet and actively strives to attain it.

This is the prime truth that religions, despite their higher caustic motivations and acts have kept alive. It is not a term used exclusively in the Christian religion, nor does it mean that you must adhere to the Christian belief system to attain this state. All ways and paths are honored if they lead a person into becoming more loving, forgiving, patient, kind, compassionate, tolerant, and happy. All paths of LOVE lead to the same Source of All That Is. We all share the same Creator-Source as living expressions of that Source Personality and we all are moving back home to unite with our Source.

Christ consciousness is the state of awareness of our true nature, our higher self, and our birthright as children of God. Christ consciousness is our living expression as a child of Spirit as we unfold our own Divine life plan onto the earth plane bringing heaven to earth. Living in the reality of our "christed" self is actually being fully alive and invested in who we truly are. In our "christed" self we live as inspiration for others to seek this for themselves so we can collectively move our planet forward into the Divine Plan for planetary transformation and glorification.

Christ became the Inspiration

And so, either way, through myth, fiction or nonfiction, the life of this man evolves as special. It is he that became the inspiration as it is the goal of human life to evolve toward Spirit. This is the journey that unfolds over the course of one's lifetime—it is the adventure of moving from time and space to eternity. Spirit ever reaches into the hearts and minds of humans to urge us to choose the ascension path to unite with the Source of

Creation. One way Spirit does this is to incarnate as a human to reveal Spirit's personality to humanity to serve as encouragement to discover and walk the path of Spirit. God as individual sparks actually steps down into the skin of a human to show us the way back home. The person who fulfilled this role was this one called Jesus who eventually inherited the name Jesus Christ.

Jesus' teachings, although not explicitly written in these bibles, is now surfacing as a new truth. These teachings centered around helping people find their own internal source of Spirit. He lived what he taught. He was the embodiment of love and goodness, peace and understanding. His God-centeredness allowed him to achieve what we consider miracles because he understood the natural laws of the universe and was able to tap into the great power of love to bring healing to people. He practiced meditation and prayer to gain strength to meet the challenges of daily life. He consistently showed love, kindness, patience, gentleness to others and encouraged them to open to the Spirit within themselves. He said, "The kingdom of Heaven is within." He lived his life to show us how to find Spirit and what a human personality looks like when he or she is Spirit-centered. He paved the way for us to find God for ourselves.

Jesus' Divine life plan apparently disclosed itself to him over the course of his lifetime. Just as we can open ourselves to our indwelling Spirits to find our own higher purpose, he had to accomplish this during his human lifetime. His story becomes an inspiring guide to help us achieve this for ourselves. Once he fully achieved his own state of "Christ Consciousness" he was able to manifest and depict to others his Divine self. His life purpose was two-fold and provides the living link between our Creator-Source and humanity: to show each person how to be God in himself/herself and for himself/herself, and then to embody the Creator and reveal God's love for each person to those who were ready to grow in Spirit.

The story as half truth

So ask yourself this: How does this god, as he is portrayed in the bibles, testaments, gospels, acts and these other proclamations of god's will really, really deep down vibrate with your own truth? Do you believe in this faith because you are simply driven to trust it regardless of science, or history, or anything?

If one attempts to make any sense to this whole mythology of the god of dominion, it becomes apparent that there are certain truths in the old stories, regardless of how scientifically or religiously absurd parts may seem. The story is really of an Old Earth that was subject to one god who required obedience, who demanded worship, who had a lot of rules to police, and who was very vengeful when people did not obey. And he had a vendetta of sin to deal with. And he obviously favored Priests and Churches as his chosen ones to administer the dominion.

If this is such a portrayal of a demanding and vengeful god who seeks obedience from the sinner, how did this myth become such an epic for billions to follow and believe? The answer resides in first, the fact that within our DNA is the quest for our God Self and a simple knowing that there is a God, a Creator of all that is. It can't be explained, it just is. Falling in love with another can't be explained, it just is, and that's the end to the discussion. The fact that the myth has a partial truth in it that rings with the heart appears to be enough to satisfy this quest of Self thus overriding all untruths. For the assumption is if there is one truth, then so must all else

47

be true. That stark truth is that *you want to* believe in the Christ Consciousness, which of course is a reflection of God even though it is not necessarily the one portrayed in this myth. It is the one already resident in you. So the truth part far outweighs the untruth and it is all simply "believed" with faith and trust because the vast majority of humanity does crave peace and love and joy.

But what if the part that is not truth is about the Son of God as he was one of many—us all? What if sin does not really exist at all, only love that cannot judge? What if the story line deletes the vengeance and need to worship and obey? What if the fear of obedience is not part of this? What if the part about Christ's birth, ascension and special powers are true and available to all. What if these demanding gods and God references are substituted by the true part of God—You? What if a new Genesis is indeed happening during these End Times—as the New Earth?

Would you want to continue to serve gods or be God? It is Your Choice.

3

THE RED PILL OR THE BLUE PILL

The biblical proliferation that rules the beliefs of billions of people holds them captive in some way to some truth that they gleam out of the mythology. And that appears to be enough. This is changing rapidly now as this other part, the bit about the vengeful, jealous, dominion seeking god just does not resonate with the expanding hearts of humanity. It is because we are in a time when the truth is surfacing and it is time to change. It is a time when the fraction of truth resident in the bibles does not outweigh the lies any more. It is a time when the untruth has to be replaced completely. So the time to simply accept that which feels amiss about a false God and these gods is over. This feeling is growing stronger and stronger as the draw to a New Genesis of New Earth is prompted into manifestation by the Christ Consciousness.

It's something you can't explain

There is a quote in the movie *The Matrix* that applies perfectly to our present time about something being "amiss". It comes when Morpheus is talking to Neo for the first time. Morpheus says:

"*I imagine right now you feel a bit like Alice, tumbling down a rabbit hole. You have the look of a man who accepts what he sees expecting never to wake up. You're here because you know something that you can't explain, but you feel it. There is something wrong with the world. You don't know what it is, but it is there, like a splinter in your mind, driving you mad. It is this feeling that has brought you to me. Do you know what I'm talking about?*"

Neo then replies with: "*The Matrix*". Then Morpheus goes on:

"*Do you want to know what it is? The matrix is everywhere, it is all around us. Even now in this very room. You can see it when you look out your window, or turn on your television set. You can feel it when you go to work, when you go to church, when you pay your taxes. It is the wool that has been pulled over your eyes to blind you from the truth. You are a slave Neo like everyone else. You were born into a prison that you cannot see, that you cannot smell, or taste or touch. A prison for your mind. Unfortunately no one can be told what the Matrix is. You have to see it for yourself. This is your last chance. After this, there is no turning back. Take the blue pill, the story ends, you wake up in your bed and believe whatever you want to believe. Take the red pill, you will stay in wonderland, and I will show you how deep the rabbit hole goes. Remember, what I am offering is the truth, nothing more. Follow me.*"

This book of **Serve gods or be God** is written because we have entered a time where these blue and red pills are before everyone, not just Neo. It is because much of what we live, what we are told by the false gods, and what we accept as a belief is not *quite* right. And when all is said and done, it is the great majority that is *not quite right.* Now I won't pretend to be Morpheus but I will say that millions of people are saying the same thing because something is amiss with them—and it is not just religions. I am the bearer of the news because I, like millions who can't really put a handle on what is wrong, know what is right, and have felt it is time to take the red pill and speak.

The difference here is that the pills are represented by a Train Ticket which requires a choice. It is the ascension trip that Jesus allegedly took to evolve the hard way. Now the train waits in a station that is going to head for the place of New Earth where things are different and Genesis 2 is happening. The reason it is waiting is for everybody to make up their minds as to whether they are willing to meet the conditions of the ticket. Where the blue pill represented the illusion of life under the deception of the financial and religious systems, this ticket is one you already have that is like the free prescription of blue pills you take every morning. You simply stay in that life which is Old Earth, hold on to your prescription, and wave goodbye to the train when it leaves, and say yes gods, I am content to serve you.

But if you take a red ticket, it's like the red pill and then a new world of truth and peace open to you as the train takes you into a magical wonderland in preparation for New Earth and your personal Christ-like Transformation.

What is a bit different here is that the depth of the rabbit hole is going to be shown to all during a special time—like Neo's training and revelation of the truth. Of course it helps if you are awake to see the new movie. Like Neo's awakening it is a time that precedes the boarding of the train and his transformation. It is a time when a new truth is presented to all equally so they understand that there is a choice and what it is. And this is the truth of God, the real one.

Now in the *Matrix* movie, Neo could take the blue pill and just go back into his dream of life in Old Earth. But this time it is not so because if you haven't picked this up yet, you should. That is the Old Earth is in a state of deterioration financially and spiritually; bankrupt one would say. And humanity, through the gods and self proclaimed agents of God who have proven to be the masters of self destruction, may not be who you want to serve anymore.

There actually is a story to this and the time of rapid disintegration that is now evident in 2011 is designed to be that way as the old energy gives way to the new. So if you think you can continue to suck up those blue pills and continue your life the way you are doing now then this may be the real fantasy.

The other dream with the red pill is the one that is kicking in as the gods (not Satan) effectively meet their Waterloo. The other dream, the new revelation, where Neo learns he is "the One" is to learn that we are all "the Ones". It is where DNA awakens, the truth comes out as to what humans really are as sentient expressions of divinity, and the dream becomes the reality. It is what the red pill, and the train ticket are all about.

So the big question is: How can you as a mere mortal gobbling these blue pills ever understand or believe in this other dream of a New Earth? That is why the train sits waiting—for you to decide. The train came into the station on March 21, 2011 and it leaves on October 28, 2011. It is the time where the choice that may be a dream becomes clear. It is the **Time of Choosing**. But there is no decision to make unless you open to knowing that there really is a believable alternative. This means you don't sleep through the new movie.

That is the point of this book. It *is* the new movie. It is to present this dream in a simple manner as to what the choice is, how it will affect your life, and why it is important for you to choose wisely during this time. It is simply up to you to believe it or not. If you want to keep chewing the old blue pills and live in fear as your financial world tumbles under the reign of the gods and those self proclaimed disciples of God, that's ok. Wave good bye to the train. But if you want to move into a world where you serve no one and learn to be God to create your own paradise, that's much better. But you must understand that at the end of the Time of Choosing, there are no more red pills or red train tickets. The train *does not* come back. Then what? Well that is what this book will tell you; as it will become clear during the Time itself—which is NOW.

Let us first talk about some prevalent prophesies that have been integrated into many belief systems on the Old Earth. In the previous chapter, it was brought out as the Book of Revelations as one example. There are many versions. These are all about what can be encapsulated into what is referred to as the End Times. And it is what those dominant religions put into those blue pills. After all, dominion over others is accomplished best when those they dominate fear something, especially god who deems all as sinful creatures. The greatest perpetrators of this have been, and still are of course the major religions who want the people to be the sheeple to believe in *their* god's word. Or? Well, as it says in the good book—vengeance will be done.

It can all be summed within three words and many, many interpretations.

Rapture, Revelation and Resurrection

Whether it is religion, New Age, or whatever, there is an absolute preponderance of information about the End Times. What are they? It's when humanity kisses their dear asses goodbye if they have not been good and have not taken their blue pills faithfully. These pills are received from the Vatican and other such institutions in return for your cost of obedience, service, faith, and trust.

The things that are going to happen during these End Times are pretty impressive. Cataclysmic events, final battles with Satan, self destruction by war and nuclear

53

means; astronomical alignments that pour rays of destruction, climatic shifts, polar shifts, magnetic reversal, global flooding, blah, blah, blah. It's the gods finally having their fill of man who is the master of self destruction and teaching them a serious lesson this time. Just type 2012 into Google and see what you get.

There is no doubt that many prophets have been responsible for this doom scenario. But those of dominion like to tell us about doom because it raises fear. Fear is what keeps the sheeple in the pen eating their blue pills.

The most popular time of this doom has been the turn of this century when all sorts of nasties were to happen as we hit these End Times. Most of the prophets like Nostradamus and Cayce screwed up on this one. But let us take some versions of End Times allegedly reflected by the words gods and God. They are always "coming". Nobody can really say what these times are and what will happen but what is important here is to understand that the End Times marks a point of change stuck in the minds of men. What is most relevant here is to understand that the End Times is a time of shift from what is Old Earth to what is to be—New Earth. It is the way it shifts that is the big controversy.

What is the old End Time?

Once more we have to enter the realm of the myths and prophesies from Old Earth that are "God" driven. In the old story of Old Earth the End Times are the time which humanity would have to make a choice. That choice would be pay for their sins and roast in Hell or choose God's word and get a reward to Heaven, eternal life, and all sorts of heavenly goodies. Or perhaps you may pay your way out by confession and repentance. And so religions, and I shall pick on the prevalent ones, have created an effective dogma around the concepts of

Revelation, Rapture, Resurrection, and Armageddon. The underlying theme, to make a simple analogy, is basically, humans, especially women, are a bunch of low life sinners and they need to make amends. They may be saved by the second coming of Christ who will reveal himself at some glorious moment. When? Perhaps when enough sinners have realized their sins and expressed absolute obedience to those representing God. And then Christ, or a Messiah, or some superhuman dude will rise and save them so they can go into heaven in eternal bliss, then sort out the rest once and for all.

In this story, **Revelation** brings together the worlds of heaven, earth, and hell in a final confrontation between the forces of good and evil. It means this is the revealing or disclosing, or making something obvious through active or passive communication with supernatural and divine entities. Of course it is believed that revelation can originate directly from a deity, or through an agent, such as an angel, most likely through the churches and religious leaders who have elected themselves the "chosen ones" that are privy to the Word of God.

The Dude that is going to disclose all this secret stuff is of course Jesus Christ, the Son of God (or the Prophet) himself. He is second in command and in for a second shot at this task to save humanity from their terrible deeds. So he is going to go through another **Resurrection** and descend back to life in a magical event worshipped as the Second Coming of Christ. As the plan unfolds, first of all he will take care of his chosen ones, then he will have a huge heavenly meeting with Dad (God), look at the tally ledger, and decide to remove all good Christians from the Earth to protect them.

This process is called Rapture, a term from the Latin verb **raptare**, and the Greek word **harpizo**, both meaning to be caught up or to be snatched up. So Jesus will snatch good Christians out of harm's way so those who have been good boys and girls can get their special treats of being saved. Those good ones are of course, the ones who have listened to the chosen ones who know the truth of the word of god and have faithfully been gobbling those blue pills, like their prescriptions are still current and paid up. Then they can be saved—lifted out of harm's way while the rest meet a different situation as their undoing dealing with the big bad guy Mr. Devil, or one of his buddies. Either way it looks pretty bad if you threw away your pills.

But listen up. Under this story there are more goodies to get if you are saved. It is about this thing of revelation which is the revealing or disclosing of life's secrets through active or passive communication with Jesus and his Pop. All those good kids will be divinely or supernaturally revealed or inspired. Revelation comes from the Greek name **Apokalypsis,** which means a disclosure, a revelation or manifestation and to be revealed. So it is a revealing of Jesus Christ himself.

In looking back at this myth, we see that this Revelation is the supposed revealing of Jesus Christ and that the message originally came from God the Father. But it was actually from god, the faker. Well, because we screwed up, especially the women, it's different. Since the introduction of sin, all communication between heaven and Earth has been terminated and has to go through Jesus Christ as he is the only mediator between this god and man. But, and here's the big but; it seems that the self elected bishops and religious gurus are the ones in between you and the gods because Christ ain't here yet. But he, of course talks to them as they are "chosen" and know the Word and what will happen and of course when. This time when this would happen was of course cleverly unstated so it could loom upon sinners forever.

And what of those poor souls that are not revealed, and snatched up? **Armageddon!** Of course there are literally hundreds of different interpretations on this as well as the Bible prophecies, especially on the issue of who is Mister Devil, the real bad guy and the battle of Armageddon. The key word here is interpretations. But you are told not to have private interpretations of prophecy at all. Why? Because god's Word gives us all we need to know without any speculation whatsoever and of course god's boys are the ones who know best.

So the bad news for those that have not been plucked out of harm's way is **Armagedon—**End Times. It will be time to pay for your sins, you bad kids. This brings the scene for the final battle between the kings of the Earth at the end of the world, a catastrophically destructive battle where Mr Satan gets his dues for meddling with the big plan for Old Earth once and for all.

And even the New Agers have something to say about this; there is a great space ship commanded by Ashtar and Sananda himself—the one who walked as Christ— waiting up there to have the equal of Scotty beam good souls to safe haven while the great battle ensues, or great catastrophes of 2012 happen.

It's a great story and the variations of this and the 2012 doomsday seems endless. And there are a lot of folks that heed to this. So they keep chewing on those blue pills, teaching their kids to eat them as well.

It is a great story that has been around in thousands of versions for some time now. And the absurdity of it as a belief system for so many "scientific", rational minds seems in itself an unbelievable fiction. And although I poke at it, this is really not funny to those who so vehemently believe it. The fear of being one of the unlucky kids who pissed off god and didn't get with his program of the "Word" means you are going to remain in harm's way and take your consequences. And so this story has been prophesized by the best BS'ers of all time—the churches and major religious leaders. And so the humans who basically want to trust someone and to seek out a true God relinquish their own beliefs to be replaced by others as their god's words.

But let us bring forward a different version of this story. For now, treat it also as a good fantasy movie.

What is the new End Time?

Since 1987, a time referred to as the Harmonic Convergence, there's been a new "buzz". It is a process of change in consciousness. What does this mean? It isn't just Neo who feels something amiss. More and more people are beginning to "think" differently about the material world, about the meaning of life, about the world around them. It's like Morpheus in the Matrix said about feeling something is not right. It is about how we relate to each other and how we relate to the Earth we live on. It's about all these gods and those kings and queens and high government officials that people gave their trust to. *Something is not right*.

Underneath more and more of our thinking time is a deep stir, a wave of desire for a better earth of peace and love. But how? It is the evolution of a different conscious awareness. Yet it still seems so unattainable. It is about a peaceful cohabitation and it began as something in the back of our minds—a sort of gut feeling from our hearts that we are being deceived from some of the crucial truths. That we may be chasing the wrong dreams and perhaps there is more to life than living in a materialistic gopher wheel serving these self proclaimed gods who love taxes, obedience, rules, and love to hoard for their own kind. But what can a mere mortal do about this? Most are trapped in the old energies because they keep chewing on the blue pills.

Many refer to this new feeling as the New Age, some the Unity Consciousness, some just the End Times. There are many names and as many ideas on this. But one thing that this new consciousness of self incorporates is that it is not an organized religion or a group. There are no leaders, no real dogma. It is some evolving awareness that has a common spiritual denominator, and it is based upon love of all things, a peaceful world of harmony that is marked by a transition time. It's a strange gut feel that something better is available.

Of course humanity likes to take this movement and make a buck in it. It is because so many have themselves made a god of ego and money. So people create great marketing ploys and devices and groups that sell you a new life, new secrets to health and wealth. It makes it hard to gain credibility this way yet despite this you cannot ever identify this movement as a dogma by a large institution like the Catholic, Protestant, or Islamic groups. It is simply an inconsistent evolution of a free spirit belief system that is pretty consistent in its beliefs.

And whether there are saviors here, great mystics, healers and wonderful products, that doesn't matter because the bottom line is that they are focused on the same dream—one of a New Earth and a new you that is more than you have believed. When you start to compile these beliefs, you begin to create a New Earth story; and it even has a storyline somewhat similar to the Old Earth storyline of rapture, revelation and resurrection.

What this boils down to is the difference between religious and spiritual, best exemplified by the dominant groups. In simple terms, religion deals with a mortal human who lives a life to serve god and his self-proclaimed cronies. He then dies beholding to the gods for his salvation into eternity. Spiritual deals with an immortal being here for the expression through temporary form of human body to express and expand love to attain joy, as an aspect of God, the Creator himself. So Religion is about serving god, Spirituality is about being God.

So what does this New Earth plan and this new consciousness movement suggest?

Well, there is a Divine Plan unfolding right before us that has never happened before. This End Time is between the turn of the century and 2012, and it has to do with various cosmic forces and planetary alignments that happen once in 26,000 years. These are forces that influence consciousness, and hence behavior. Of course everyone has a choice as to whether they let this new consciousness into their awareness to create new behavior. Needless to say, you have free will and choice to decide, just like you decide to eat the blue pills.

But at any rate, during this shift into the new 26,000 year cycle—called the Age of Aquarius—there is commonality to certain things that are going to happen that shower a new "knowing" into the consciousness of humanity. It is a dramatic acceleration of what Neo felt and what so many are feeling.

Yes, another version of the religious story. Now bear in mind that what I am about to tell you is not mainstream New Age stuff. It is a New Earth story.

Revelation is indeed the revealing or disclosing, or making something obvious through active or passive communication with supernatural and divine entities. This time, the **Revelation** originates directly from the Source. Yes, God—the real One—directly to you and into your personal consciousness, not through anyone else. There are no middle men to tell you what the word of God is because you begin to understand that it is you that is the "chosen one" already privy to the truth of God.

But it is not going to be disclosed by Jesus himself. It is *you* that is going to go through a **Resurrection** and all who so choose to believe this will resurrect themselves coming back to a re-life as the Second Coming of Christ. It is not one guy, it is all!

So there are no chosen ones after a big meeting deciding to remove all Christians from the Earth, to protect them. This **Rapture** is simply your own choice when you understand that you are something else than what you have been told to believe as a mortal human. So Jesus will not "snatch us" out of harm's way if we have been good. It is you that simply decides a new way. For under this story good and bad are judgments and love cannot and does not judge. Thus, there is no judgment. It's like a mother who truly loves her kid; regardless of what the little monster does, she loves him and does not judge. It is the other people who judge and may force her to action—the consciousness of others prevails.

Then the goodies you get through **Revelation** are indeed the revealing or disclosing, through active or passive communication of who you really are—an aspect of God, an eternal being borrowing a body to experience a time slice on Earth. And this is where a common denominator of vibration fits in. You vibrate higher and higher, releasing many of those miraculous abilities that Jesus Christ himself had—especially the healing. So you can look at this as a mass revealing of Jesus Christ through the consciousness shift. But it is *not* Jesus suddenly appearing. It is the Time of Revelation when the *knowing* of this, and in many cases, the *showing* of this (as he did), is revealed.

So we see that this Revelation is the revealing of Jesus Christ as being each of us and that the message now comes directly from God the Father as a wakeup call of rapture. And it is a revealing that there is no sin and that the heaven we seek is already within us as immortal, eternal aspects of God. So it is a call not to serve gods, or listen to other's interpretations of God's Word, but to BE God and know for yourself. The revealing is that you don't need gurus, bishops, meditators or the likes to tell you the secrets of heaven, being eternal and how to have a better life. It is simply the acceptance of who you are that is already living a life as a Spiritual entity borrowing a body to be within rather than a body looking for spirit outside of itself.

And what of those poor souls that do not want to believe or accept this? Well here we go again. **Armageddon.** Which one? Guess what? It's the one you are in now. The one that creates fear, conflict, with a drive of ego to survive and dominate. It is called the world of separation from who you are. Now interestingly enough, this Armageddon changes as all this shifts in consciousness toward 2012.

Is there bad news here? Is there something that happens to those who want to believe in their old ways? What if you choose to take the path that this is just all more dogmatic horseshit with a new color?

What about those that have not chosen to believe who they are? It is indeed being left in your own harm's way and guess what? Yes, **Armagedon**—End Times. You continue paying for your sins of hatred and separation and conflict and fear as you are doing right now. It becomes a clear understanding of how *you* attract that which you create. Is it hard to believe that if you hate people they will hate you back? It wasn't God that did this, it was you. It is you that attracts it by the energy you create; the big difference is that energy in the Old Earth will not be inflicted upon anyone else like it was in the old regime. And get this; through the End Times it will manifest itself to return faster and faster until it becomes instant.

That is the true Armageddon where you create your own Hell at your own choosing, and of your own intensity. Is the fight with Mr. Devil in the cards here? It sure is if you want to hold to the old ways of deception and greed that you want to inflict on others! Your fight is with yourself—the Devil is within.

And **rapture**? The only people that are going to get snatched out of their own devils (harm's way) are the ones that choose to understand who they are—and the snatching is of their own accord.

So this is not a big battle between Satan and the kings of the Earth as the end of the world dawns. It is a battle of your own mind, of who you are. It is about your own conscious awareness and belief that you will do battle with. It is about the knowing that you will inflict upon your mortal being to create your own life. The battle of Armageddon is a battle of belief in yourself. Do you keep chewing the blue pills or not. Indirectly this is indeed a conscious choice of Heaven or Hell.

That's a pretty simple choice is it not? Heaven or Hell? Perhaps not if you are stuck in the old world?

Let us bring in another old over-used term of **Crucifixion.** In the End Times it is the process of crucifying what is Hell by leaving it behind and choosing Heaven. It is the death of the old in choice of the new. Even on Old Earth, everyone, yes everyone, has a choice of how (bad or good) they perceive any situation. And when you learn that what you perceive as you think, speak feel and act upon brings upon you like energy, you may pay more attention to what you think and do. That is what the Train Ticket on the Ascension Train is all about. The train ticket says: *"Ok, I have had enough with this Old Earth and I want to live a life of unconditional love, peace and joy."* And by acceptance, just like a commercial contract, it is so enacted by your intent.

So the story is similar but with a different twist from what the dominant religions tell you.

Is this another dogma? Well, it ain't written by God in an autographed hard cover. It ain't on the evening news. And it certainly ain't supported by any religion. And there ain't no leaders. But it is unfolding all around everyone at the same time if you have the eyes, ears and heart to open to this revelation. What follows in the book is simply information about what IS happening. You cannot make a choice if there is no alternative known to you.

So here is your challenge; read this as a fantasy version if you like. It is no more fantasy than Genesis or Moses parting the Red Sea, or Noah's Ark. Then look around you and listen to what's happening and what you feel in your heart. You can't BS the heart and this may lead you to burning the prescription for blue pills.

At this time in this evolution, we sit in the Time of Choosing that would be the Revelation. It started on March 21st, 2011 and ends on Oct 28, 2011. It is tied to what is known as the Mayan 9th wave of Unity Consciousness. This is when you get your train ticket to New Earth.

It's when you decide to serve gods or be God. It is your choice.

4

THE END TIMES or THE BEGINNING?

The new version of the End Times includes the transition from the Old Earth to the New Earth. The time of transition has been commonly portrayed as the time from the turn of the century 1999 to 2012. On Old Earth it was not fashionable to talk about metaphysics. Physics was the buzz, not esoteric things. If you really care to study quantum physics you will quickly realize that it explains metaphysics whereas physics cannot. The main reason that quantum physics has had such a tough time getting entrenched is because there is one component of it that the scientists still (after 80 years) argue about: Consciousness. Consciousness is the missing link to how it all works.

On New Earth it is quite fashionable to talk about metaphysics because physics is outdated. It cannot see beyond the observer's observations as quantum physics teaches us. Physics cannot deal with or create laws of behavior on those tiny particles that are not subject to gravity. Gravity is the glue to hold material things together. It is what we know under Newtonian physics as "solid" things made of atoms held by gravity. But consciousness is the glue that creates things in the quantum world. So if you think you know it all as a Newtonian scientist that has been trained to observe what you see, knowing the other 90% is made of stuff you can't see, then how can you know it all?

The transition from Old to New Earth is also exemplified by the old TV and news media systems versus the new media system of the Internet. If you dare to type in some esoteric or metaphysical topic in Google you will get millions upon millions of news items, research and discussions that come forward. Before the year 2000 it was not like that. Something has taken hold on the conscious attention to create this shift. Now it is like a tsunami of shifting thought—a building energetic field of common attention and awareness. What's this all about?

Well, there is some hard science here. It's all about this big grand cycle of 26,000 years where our solar system passes through the point of alignment with the center of the galaxy. This is the Grand Alignment in 2012. In fact there are a whole lot of things happening up there that are grand—different than ever before. It is all astronomical data that you can check out for yourself. And at the end of this 26,000 year cycle that has been mostly relegated to importance by those weird metaphysicists is this last tiny little period that started in 1999 and ends in 2012.

The Mayan End Times

There is a big buzz these days on the Internet and in bookstores about the Mayan Calendar. It is not clearly understood how these Mayans received this information, nor how it applies to humanity now, but nevertheless it is infusing into the new consciousness as a new truth. It is important to understand that this is not a prophesy of physical doom and destruction, it is a revealing of a process of behaviour and evolution of consciousness.

Regardless of whether it is of plant, animal or man, it is the consciousness that orchestrate the will to survive and the life attitude.

It is particularly focussed on the End Times as these Mayans allegedly took old ancient knowledge and advanced it as their science. First they were very focused on the cosmic movements and nature because the Sun provided light for life to exist. As the Earth provided nourishment to grow, the planets provided the seasons as well as the consciousness mood of the Earth. These they observed carefully and recorded as their own "Days" and "Nights" with different underlying moods and purposes affecting not only nature but all that lives. They saw this change the mood of the people as well. But more important to them was they needed food. So they learned to pay attention to these moods of the universe to survive.

The Mayan calendar therefore reflects the movement of these cosmic cycles of Day and Night, seasons and growth behaviour of all life. They determined there were 13 periods called Heavens. These were a way of describing the phases of growth found in all that lives. For example, from when a seed is planted, there are 7 Days and 6 Nights each with a specific purpose each with different lengths depending on what "Underworld" they belong to (see later). Note that these Days and Nights were not like our 24 hour night and day, although they based these on cyclical patterns of celestial objects like the Sun. These they called the 13 Heavens alternating from Day to Night, each affecting the process of natural growth from seeding to eventual flowering and re-seeding.

The first Heaven is Day 1, the *sowing* time when a seed is planted. The second Heaven, or Night 1, is the time of *inner assimilation* when it readies for transforming itself in preparation for the third Heaven of Day 2, of *germination* when it begins to develop within Mother Earth to reach towards the Sun. There is then Heaven 4, or Night 2 of *resistance* as it must gain its power and internal sustenance to force through to see the Sun. You begin to see how the Day is one of expansion while the night is one of resistance or adjustment, each at a different phase of the growth. It is the mood of Mother Earth that can affect this growth towards its fulfillment, as can the Sun which to them was the Father.

The next Heaven 5, Day 3 is when it *sprouts*, the first time to emerge to see Father Sun and now the Earth and the Sun work together to provide nourishment below and life energy above to the new plant. As it begins to grow, it must adjust itself to the new world around it and *assimilate* through the Heaven 6, Night 3, to adjust itself properly. As it so does, it enters the Heaven 7, next Day 4 which is to *proliferate* itself through the new energy of the Sun. It then enters the next Heaven 8, Night 4 as it attempts to *expand* itself to be what it was meant to be.

During the Heaven 9, Day 5 it is the time of *budding* for its main purpose to produce. Heaven 10, Night 5 is a time of destruction as the plant now must place all of its energy into producing its flower if it is to flourish. Of course, Heaven 11, Day 6 is when the plant flourishes into *flowering*. Heaven 12, Night 6 is when it must *fine tune* itself to blossom to its fullest, and finally Heaven13, Day 7 is the *fruition* when its bounty in the of form seeds is completed. Each Heaven is dependent on the mood of the Sun and Mother Earth as to what they can provide to support the growth to maturity.

Each Day and Night brings a new phase of challenge and growth as its very purpose, and its essence towards its final purpose change. The elements of fire, earth, water, and air are all vital to the success, as are the internal abilities of the plant to grow. Its will to live and survive is its very essences or spirit. They saw this as its consciousness. Their wisdom taught that all life abides by this. All life including man whose essences are his consciousness are influenced by the moods of the cosmos, and the Sun and the Earth whether they understand it or not.

It is because the essence of man, the consciousness is part of the God of all that exists. It, like the Mother Earth, and the Sun are all living things which are themselves going through the same phases. All of life behaves according to this grand plan. All are subject to their influences as they change their positions around us. Just as they determine the way a seed will grow, they determine the way a man will grow and mature, and develop his own essence.

What they also determined was that there were a whole set of other time periods in their calendar called Underworlds. Each period is itself a stage of complete evolution on a larger scale. The period of 13 Heavens is an Underworld. There are 9 Underworlds of different lengths. The shortest is the Universal Underworld of 260 days (our days). The next longest is the Galactic Underworld which is 20 times longer than the Universal, and so on. Again, each Underworld is made up of the 13 Heavens. At the start of each one, a major level of evolution in consciousness starts then goes through the 13 Heavens maturing progressively like the plants.

When the end phase of each Underworld is reached, meaning the 13th Heaven of *Fruition*, a new Underworld that is twenty times shorter in length begins as the First Day of sowing. It is like when one Underworld produces a seed that can then go through the Heavens twenty times faster. Thus during the last period of the Planetary 7th Day, the seeding of the First Day in the Galactic period may occur. At the last 7th Day in the Galactic, a new seed is created to be sown to begin the Universal period. When all 9 Underworlds are complete, a new period where there is no time begins. Each one has a specific consciousness function and sets the foundation for the next shorter one (20 times shorter). And they all end at the same time. That is what the Mayans saw as the End Times as their calendar ceased and went into a period of no time.

What is relevant here is that all 9 of these Underworlds (or waves) except this last one called *Universal* (260 days) has reached the 13th Heaven. And all 9 waves end on October 28, 2011. The one underneath this one, the *Galactic* Underworld, is 12.8 years long and we have entered its last 13th Heaven of *Fruition* as have all others. It sits on a bigger one 20 times longer and so on.

It is this last one of 260 days that is of interest as it began on March 9, 2011 and terminates *Fruition* on October 28, 2011. Recently this has been adjusted by the experts on this to 18 of our days for each Heaven to total 234 days. What is notable is that there is an acceleration as time speeds up. What this means is that the aspect of consciousness pertaining to each Heaven speeds up its evolution by 20 times for each Underworld which we will call a wave. In other words, as much as we learned in the last wave of 12.8 years will be learned in the current wave of 234 days.

This Universal Underworld is the final transformation of consciousness and it is what is referred to as the 9th Wave.

The prophesy about these End Times when these all end together is that this is a great change in the consciousness of humanity as they approach the fruition of all Underworlds. It will be a time when the consciousness of man has no association with time. It is the time of the revealing and the entry to a new age as the rebirth starts from the seed of the last underlying Underworld. At that time the world is without time and consciousness of man would have evolved to its ultimate point of fruition. This means it is up to those who are left to start creating the new world and the new civilization. It will be a period where man will be one with nature and Mother Earth and the Solar system will come into galactic synchronization with the rest of the Universe. Those left will be transformed as they pass through the center of the cosmos. All will be One and the material will be balanced with spirit. It was called Hunab Ku in Mayan. It is referred to as the Unity Consciousness.

The Ninth Wave—what is it?

The 9th wave is the final wave which rests upon the final Fruition stages of all 8 waves. It is the culmination of all consciousness, setting the final stage for the time when there is no time after the Grand Alignment of Dec 21, 2012 when Earth passes through the center of the Galaxy. Essentially, these waves get shorter and shorter until there is no time, only instant by instant. Its purpose is to bring in the final step of unity consciousness. It is all about setting a consciousness mood that we are all One. And it is about revealing that being all One, there is within us a divine aspect as we are One with the Creator, as we are one with Creation. That spark of us referred to as our Light Body, that invisible quantum overlay on the physical atomic body, is what is said to be a piece of God.

This Grand Alignment, and a whole lot of other unique celestial configurations occur through 2012, after the 9th wave completes in 2011. It creates the setting for the final transformation of resurrection. These waves are the ones that have been evolving the unity consciousness and are meant to set the underlying consciousness like an overlay from above so that it sets the tone—or garden—for manifestation and creation below. In our terms of reference this is from 5D and 4D above to 3D below. It sets the tone of the Resurrection.

It is important to understand what is meant as "D". It is not a mathematical terminology. These terms will be used a lot here: 1D, 2D, 3D reflects matter as physical earth and our bodies (Newtonian physics of atoms), 5D being non-matter or etheric quantum space, and 4D as the space between (Quantum physics of waves).

The 13 Heavens reflected the stages of growth, alternating from female (nurturing) to male (protection) energies, alternating between day and night, each having an energetic influence as they determined was ruled by gods which had certain powers and attributes to affect that stage of growth. They, as all humanity, have created many gods and deities who they worship as their idols and have assigned special powers to them. It is simply humanity's DNA calling as this is encoded to seek God within; which has through lower vibrations become seeking god without. In this case, what they could not understand and respected they called gods.

At each Heaven of Day and Night, just as the growing conditions of above (Father Sun) and Below (Mother Earth) set the tone for optimum growth, of nurturing and adjustment, so does the prevailing mood of consciousness set the tone for the strength, clarity of intent (seed) so as to provide optimum growth into fruition—that being the intent of humanity to manifest and create in 3D what has been seeded and nurtured in consciousness of 5D.

How to best align with this tone is to understand the nature of the process of growth and expansion at each phase. In the case of seeds, it is the nourishment of dark soil and water that vitalizes, whereas when sprouting, it is the sun and the nutrients that are needed. In the case of consciousness, it is the balanced female/male love from the divine heart that nurtures and integrates into the new form. Thus every Day and Night is "charged" with specific frequencies of care and attention of that stage, looking for that which provides it. It is as the stage of growth in a child, where the father and mother shift their attention to the needs of the child as it matures. By aligning with the needs, the process of growth matures with vigor and strength at each stage—all set into the fundamental nourishment of love.

HEAVEN	DAY/NIGHT	ENERGY	TIME
1	Day 1	Sowing	Mar 9 - Mar 26
2	Night 1	Inner assimilation of new wave	Mar 27- Apr 13
3	Day 2	Germination	Apr 14 - May 1
4	Night 2	Resistance against new wave	May 2 -19
5	Day 3	Sprouting	May 20 - June 6
6	Night 3	Assimilation of new wave	June 7- 24
7	Day 4	Proliferation	June 25 - July 12
8	Night 4	Expansion of New Wave	July 13 - 30
9	Day 5	Budding	Jul31 - Aug 17
10	Night 5	Destruction	Aug 18 - Sept 4
11	Day 6	Flowering	Sep 5 - 22
12	Night 6	Fine tuning of new Protoform	Sep 23 - Oct 10
13	Day 7	Fruition	Oct 11 - 28
Each Heaven is 18 earth days long			

At the end of these 9 waves, the total consciousness of humanity and the universe is set to blossom permanently in Unity. It is the year 2012 that the unity consciousness, truly emerges and blossoms into the 3D reality having been implanted in the garden of consciousness of 5D to be expressed in the reality of 3D. It is so for those that choose to be planted in the light of the garden of love through the Time of Choosing that is the 9th wave and the Time of Revelation. Then these celestial bodies and energies gifted from the Galactic Center as we approach in 2012 do their final fine tuning of total consciousness. This will be the Resurrection or the final Time of Transformation. And what is it that results? First is the shift in consciousness to unity and that consciousness is what materializes the New Earth.

The Divine Plan

Now I am going to bring to you a bit of news that reflects the enormous wave that dominates the New Earth energies. It's a prophesy that has the bottom line of all the millions of opinions of what is happening and what was meant to happen with regard to this End Time and The Grand Alignment and the big cycle of 26,000 years. It is about the transformation through our new version of Revelation and Resurrection. It is this that we will cover in the next chapters. Again, you can get many opinions on this but there is a common denominator. Here is the simplified version.

The Divine Plan has been to allow Gaia (Gaia is Mother Nature) and Earth to ascend (to ascend means to rise in vibration so as to live in a body form without having to die—as your eternal self as part of God) at this special time but the overall Divine Plan is and always was to allow all that choose to ascend so as to bring the aspect of the God Self to lower form; to experience and to expand the joy of its wonder. At this point it is the time of Gaia and Earth's ascension to be completed with the alignment of galactic center which is her origin. She and earth have offered themselves in sacrifice to be the body and form of the Great Experiment of souls to bring all things upon her and connected to her into the evolution of spirit. It is her destiny and it is her members of the Cosmic Council (the planets that the Mayas deemed as gods) that assist in this as they pour their love and their aspects of unique vibrations upon her and all things upon her.

The Divine Plan has been for humanity to be allowed to ascend with her by their own free will—God's gift to all should they choose to ascend and to recognize the power of love. The overall choice for Gaia's humanity was to be determined by the overall vibration of Earth and her inhabitants. It had to reach a certain threshold and so it did during the period referred to as the Harmonic Convergence of 1987. The question was whether humanity could earn this right of ascension that Gaia was to engage in regardless. Otherwise, Gaia would ascend by herself. And so it trigged the Divine Plan which originally was to place within the design of all, the knowing of the God Self and the attributes of Creator and Creation. It would be there in all equally, and placed as a spark of quest of Self and Home as accessed through the heart, the seat and power of the Divine Self. It was the time of the Harmonic Convergence that showed humanity had earned this right.

And so it was encoded within the DNA, placed within each, in a place where it could never be lost. It would be within each heart as the gateway to find the way to this truth and to allow this gate to open to bring it forward into consciousness. It is the Divine Plan to allow each and all to grow, evolve and express the joy of love and to receive love and bliss. In return one could learn to ascend in form and to make greater and expand the totality of love of the Creator as the supreme force of all that is. It is what Christ did—the hard way. It is the Divine Plan to allow all possibilities in all beings equally and to create by free will that which they desire to attain joy. The process would be first in thought above, then to form material below, all released by the essence of pure unconditional love—the glue of all that is.

The Divine Plan is to allow creation with the tools of love through the gateway of the heart. And as humanity has shown its worthiness in love, so it is that the Divine Plan is now manifesting upon Gaia and Earth, into new form in wondrous expansion of the universe which is God's mind.

The New Earth: GENESIS II

And so God looked at his creation and pondered it. He called his eldest Son and his Daughter forward as Co-Creators.

"We have seen the evolution of the Old Earth and we have seen how all of your brothers and sisters have lived upon it. It has been a time when the spirit was allowed to be under dominion of the egos, and so it has been. Now we are seeing that humanity is bringing forward this spirit which we have quietly placed within them. It is a time to consider the New Genesis of New Earth as we shall conceive and give birth to. We see that your brother Christ has indeed left a legacy of spirit and that it has not been subjugated and it is still alive for all.

It is a time that your brothers and sisters have earned their rights to know of themselves. This time we will allow the spirit to come forward in those that have chosen and New Earth can be once again a perfect world that will be inhabited by the ones who choose. It was as we had on Old Earth but it evolved away from spirit of true self to grow and know. Let us once again create a new Genesis and allow the goodness of Old Earth to meld into the New Earth. This Genesis will be formed from the consciousness of those brothers and sisters that awaken, and we will so present them with the gift of ascension into the New Earth."

For the billions that already believe in Genesis, or some form of it, such a proposal from God (the real one of Love) should not be difficult. What is different about this one is that it is totally based upon our Higher Beings, not the egos as the little gods within each of us.

Let me lay upon you some insight to the New Earth that is forming in the 4D ethers of consciousness as a result of the shift during the End Times. Through the seeding of the new unity consciousness of the last wave the seeding by way of pure intent and love, humanity are planting into the ethers of pure love the blueprint and construct for the New Earth. It is here the concept of form and purpose is created that precedes the conception which through the purity of divine male and female are conceived into creation.

This is about the melding of three elements through the intent of unity consciousness; the pure New Earth as a 5D concept of intent of pure consciousness, as the melding of physical purity; the alignment of cosmic forces and planets; and the overlay of the purity of love manifestation of that which is heaven. This is the concept like Genesis that is conceived in the joint minds and is birthed as an egg of union of male and female as equal divine energies.

This seeding of New Earth then follows the process of the 9th wave into temporary energy of 4D which may be likened to the gestation of the New Earth, ending at the Dec 21st Solstice/Equinox of 2011 shortly after the Time Of Choosing. It is the formation or congealing into 4D of the model of New Earth, ready to receive its inhabitants that have so chosen to evolve through the final stage of evolution from 3D to 5D for them and from 4D to 3D for New Earth.

During the year 2012 the shift of the process of transformation into 3D will occur as the cosmic forces of ascension shower upon those chosen to move with Gaia, and Gaia herself. These particular frequencies will act as triggers to activate the DNA antenna and receivers. This new form, like the chrysalis opening will show itself more and more to those aware at and after the time of the Venus Transit in June of 2012. It then begins to congeal into the New Earth. And so the 3D representation of the hologram will be born at the time of the great alignment of Dec 21, 2012, in preparation for the great resurrection of the New Earth. It will be so within the total unity consciousness of God and the Christ Consciousness.

Then with the cosmic configuration of forces and planets, when the New Earth has shifted from the 5D concept, to 4D conception to manifestation and creation in 3D reality, it will be ready to accept souls who have chosen to move into that reality. Of course by that time the Great Revelation (Time of Choosing) and the Great Resurrection (Time of Transformation of Ascension) will have readied those for the shift to the New Earth reality.

It is the Time of Transformation that physicality begins to congeal into new form, both for Gaia, the New Earth, and humanity that chooses to ascend with her. The separation of Old and New Earth will become a conscious reality and the final formation will be after the Earth, like humanity, has been gifted the cosmic forces and overlays that will be completed by the time of 3D birth. From then on, again, like in a newborn child, the configuration of the stars, the contracts each are creating now, and the movements of the Cosmic Gods of creation will guide the evolution of the New Earth. And the New Beings linked between realities of 3D-5D will emerge, then evolve into the next age of unconditional love over 26000 years, spilling their presence into the Galaxies.

So is it the end or the beginning? Do you want to serve the gods of Old Earth or be God on New Earth? You choose.

We are now back to that Train Ticket bound for New Earth. But you don't have to take it yet; remember there are some conditions. Let us explore in more detail how this story is meant to unfold during these two critical times of Revelation and Resurrection.

5

REVELATION-THE TIME OF CHOOSING

The current Time of Choosing

It is hard to conceive on how this story of New Earth Genesis is to unfold in such a short time. And admittedly there are as many opinions on this as there are people. This chapter is to bring more detail to you of the Time of Choosing when the Revelation occurs. As already covered, on March 21, 2011 a special window of time opened which is referred to as The Time of Choosing. It can be likened to the Old Earth Time of Revelation. It is not the one that the religions are attempting to put the fear of God into people about. It is the one that the religions have feared would take away their powers of dominion. This particular time parallels the 9th Wave of Unity Consciousness.

The Divine Plan will further unfold as the next major part of the Unity Consciousness evolution comes forward to all humanity. The way in which humanity receives this, or reacts to it, will not be known as it is an individual choice that determines the individual path. However, one can identify the major influences of this plan. Parts of the higher attributes of each DNA field have already opened but they, like all else, will await self awareness and intent. The next major opening of DNA will occur near the summer solstice of 2011 and open fully the 12 layers. This will be covered later. But the final God Self layer will not open fully until the cosmic trigger of the Venus Transit in 2012.

Through the Time of Choosing, many cosmic influences will pour onto Earth. The blue-white light from the Central Sun, energies from planetary alignments, from the heart of Creator, and special rays of the cosmos are but a few, all of which will intensify. The blue-white light is the light energy that is responsible for the transformation of matter in line with the Divine Plan. The opened DNA, acting like a receiving antenna, will receive these energies to transmute signals through the chakra system into the physical chemistry, as well as further opening the DNA.

At the same time, the consciousness of humanity and Gaia will also respond. And the Cosmic Council described as the celestial planetary bodies will align and radiate in accordance with their roles in the Divine Plan of ascension. The cosmic bodies are planets and stars that themselves have unique frequencies to transmit and attune into the process. The cosmic triggering mechanism will orchestrate influences through this Time of Choosing as the DNA receivers open and act in response, in total harmony with the Divine Plan. The showering of new energy will open up higher functions, chakras, DNA attributes, awareness and knowing, all culminating in total unity consciousness of love as the prevailing earth energy, ready for the New Earth.

There are stages to this process. The first through the Time of Choosing is a small dose to affect the beginning of the transformation and the shift in the knowing of all. The second stage is where the intensity is increased successively to affect the Time of Transformation, or

Resurrection. It will change consciousness in accordance with the 9th wave Days and Nights.

Although the reaction of individuals rests to free choice, all of humanity will be affected in some way by this the same way the Unity Consciousness has developed as the underlying mood. Regardless, through free choice, this mood can simply be overridden. The area of knowing will heighten to allow the consciousness of peace, love and unity to prevail. It will over-light darkness and create the means in the many to feel and see the energy changes in others so there will be nowhere for darkness to hide. The cosmic rays broadcasting from above will also fill the magnetic grid systems around the planet and flow over into 3D communications systems; as a new knowing of what is happening and why it is so will become the top priority of millions upon millions of people. A new knowing of what is happening will take over.

And minions of ascended ones will be revealed and come forward, awaiting this time to align with and amplify the new energy of ascension. As the cosmic triggers occur and impact DNA, the attributes of healing, of telepathy, of all those attributes that have been deemed nonsense by science will suddenly make a mockery of science and the shift will become undeniable even to the most stubborn 3D human.

Medicine, communications, science, history, old schools will begin to be seen like the silly narrow visions of humans stuck in old ways. The energy of deception, control and dominion, of greed and selfishness will lose substance and the majority will know or feel through new senses when others carry such energies. The aspect of the Divine Plan will show itself as the Unity Consciousness brings millions to the same truth. In conjunction with this there will be heightened drama in resistance as individuals who would continue to impose darkness without consent or to harm others. They will not be able to project this energy; and instead they will receive it upon themselves, faster and faster, and stronger and stronger.

All manifestation will quicken and individuals will quickly realize that they are creators of these energies being returned. And the knowing of how energy works under the law of ascension will become revealed to all. And those who choose to ignore this will fall to their own designs to bring upon themselves more negative drama. Of greatest significance during this time will be the knowing of truth, through the dispersion of both above and below what is occurring as the law of as above, so below becomes undeniable. And when the main events unfold, purpose will become known and why a choice is at hand.

The unity of the messages will ring throughout humanity through the meridians and magnetic grids of Gaia and the universe, into the etheric fields and vibrate in the DNA of humanity as one entrains the other. The energy of new truth will show itself as a disabling energy that will affect that which has been constructed in darkness and not of the light. By the time of the Time of Choosing's end in October, the majority of humanity will simply know, or know of, the Divine Plan. All of humanity will have a need to make a choice and many may resist. Some may cling to old ways but they will become the odd ones and will begin to be told of, or see, their folly.

The major systems of Earth that are based upon the old energy of separation and deception will begin to lose their grounding and the support of these will wane as humanity shifts attention. The two most prevalent forces that have been controlled by dark energies are the financial and religious structures, one based upon the deception of debt, the other in the deception of true self. These will lose their hold and fail as new energies flood in to replace them. Thus the truth of the bible system will begin to take precedence, thus enfolding and dissolving that which is not truth.

In addition, the ways of men upon Old Earth and Gaia will be reminded of their folly, so as to nurture the need for change. Old ways such as the use of nuclear power (Japan) will be recipients of physical reaction that will point to a need for humanity to take action to alternative ways of power and use of energy in harmony with the Earth. This will show itself in drama where a concentration of deception and old ways misalign with the ways of New Earth. This is not meant as punishment, for all are eternal beings above physical death. It is all unfolding as part of the Divine Plan.

It is here in this time that those who are advanced in this progression will serve to assist the others who are not. It is to assist these souls that require the knowing of choice, of the light, of a better way. It is a knowing that divinity speaks loud and clear and resistance will become overbearing as it will affect the individual so resisting. It is not as a threat but as an understanding of what they already do unknowingly with their own energies of manifestation; but now in accelerated mode. It is to know and act on new ways of harmony with all that is and to not be led by those who have ruled under the old separation consciousness.

All this will flourish through enhanced abilities in others that will be recognized and shown openly. It is this that will help others understand they are themselves the victims of their own doings; and that none of the negative world is necessary. That free will is always there to choose. By the end of the Time of Choosing there can be no hidden agendas. The Divine Plan is to be revealed first and foremost so all can know and become what they are. And the knowing of the truth will prevail as the dominant consciousness. The new Unity Consciousness will be focused on knowing and showing and it will so lay the foundation for the infusion of the true Christ Consciousness.

The free ride on the Ascension Train

During the Time of Choosing the Ascension Train awaits a decision. It is a train that leads to the ultimate physical transformation and train station upon New Earth. The Time of Revelation to bring light to the awareness and rising of Spirit and Divine Love.

After the Time of Choosing, there will be a closure of the affairs revealing all, to fully blossom as *Fruition* through the 9th wave as the Great Revelation. It is the time when the Unity Consciousness and divinity shout loud and clear to humanity that this planet is shifting to a new age of ascension and that it is time to board the New Earth train.

The tickets are given freely by way of awareness, acceptance, and intent. For if the new energy of love and unity is not purposely chosen over the old energies of separation there can be no ticket to board the train which leaves at the end of the Time of Choosing on October 28 of 2011. Intent is the most powerful of energies and it is the requirement of allowing the final evolution in the purity of love. Otherwise the destination—the next phase of Resurrection cannot be.

The 9th wave sets the foundation in 2011 for Resurrection in 2012. It sets the platform for DNA to allow the physical 3D evolution. It is this time that the full intensity of the Cosmic Forces and the blue-white energy from Source begins its transformation. This is the second coming of Christ, but it is not one man, it is humanity rising together into the unity consciousness brought to 3D physicality by allowing the DNA to do its work, translating the cosmic forces into the physical below aligning with the individual intent. This time, unlike any other, allows all to rise in Christ Consciousness together. It is an unstoppable, undeniable process preparing for the resurrection of the divinity in all that so choose. This sets the stage for a physical 3D manifestation and it is the result of choice during the 9th

wave that allows this to be. It is awareness, choice and intent that are the trigger—and the New Earth train ticket.

The orchestration of this emergence of the new human is like a butterfly from a cocoon, as the energies above and below align to provide the energy of transformation of the chrysalis body that has contained the physics and the spirit. At all stages, it is fed externally by cosmic forces of transformation, and internally by acceptance of the truth of divinity—all alive in a unity consciousness of love. Each stage builds upon the previous and it is the succession of these brought at a special time at the end of the Age that allows this to be. If awareness and intent is not used as the trigger to allow, then the receiving falls upon vessels and vehicles that cannot complete the transformation. It would be like not turning on your device, so it cannot receive, nor transfer its messages.

The process of resurrection begins with the process of revelation and through the catalyst of free choice and will; the intent allows the unique cosmic forces to conclude the final transformation of Gaia and humanity. So the choice of boarding the New Earth train is lost at the end of Revelation, the closing, because consciousness is not ready. And hence the destination is not attainable because the vehicle to receive and allow is not receptive at the times scheduled in the resurrection. It is free will that prevails.

This is what those who have chosen can assist on—to be in service and love so the knowing of Choice is brought to awareness and is clear to those that flounder, or cling to old ways. It is to open the light where darkness hides, to assist those who desire a love filled, peaceful life as a Creator; to assist them in their tickets so as to open to Resurrection with grace and ease. It is so as many souls as possible can receive the divine gift and can walk the New Earth as they were meant to. Never before has this ever occurred.

It is not a time of Judgment

The choice to take the ticket to Resurrection is not a judgment of God at the pearly gates, nor a decision of man or gods to allow any one on board. It is not determined by the level of vibration but it is important to understand that the level of vibration (I will explain level of vibration later), the awareness of self, the engagement in love in all affairs are highly important as they quicken and make easier the transformation through resurrection as it becomes a wonderful, wondrous experience of love and transmutation. The higher the vibration, the more receptive is the being and the forces that are gifted to do this allow it to be experienced swiftly with grace and ease to shift and unfold the true flower of your being. It is the ticket that is given freely in unconditional love as a gift of God— free, received by pure intent alone with the understanding written upon it that there will be change, there will be a New Earth, and there will be ascension based upon unconditional love of Source, one hologram with only peace, love, joy eternal. The ticket is given upon acceptance. All others on the train will be of service to each other to assist regardless of state of vibration.

The energy is shifting

And what of the old Earth energies? It is an understatement to say that many of the Old Earth energy structures are dissolving in this time of Choosing and Revelation creating stress for many. It is because they are not necessary to the higher world and serve no purpose, and most important they are contrived vehicles of dominion and deception—void of unconditional love, the essence of high vibration.

The control mechanisms that have grown to be dominated by profit, control, and greed are being exposed by the light that is shining upon them. This will place pressure on those who depend on the government, banking, medical, employment, and pension systems based on deception and control. The truth about religious systems and truth with regards to the inner world, extra terrestrials, and about people's spiritual powers will become more common. Many will resist this, ignore it, fear the change, cling to old energies and perhaps even resort to conflict. Those that deceive most will have the greatest adjustment as their energies wane.

It can be a trying time for many rooted in the old energies of dependence and polarity. Some will leave, some will adjust, some will awaken, but many will be bewildered as to what to do. This is the final adjustment phase of the evolution, but many will evolve as strong to show others the way. This is where many will develop manifesting and co-creation skills to help others do the same through the rough times. Healing skills will open to be stronger and stronger. This is the way to have others pay attention. Many will begin to realize the worthlessness of the outer world and move inside, support relationships, and learn to change their attention as the light increases and attraction/manifestations become faster. All have had equal light shone upon them but many will simply be oblivious to this.

The shift in power

The Time of Choosing is about the true source of power. It has shifted for millions now and it is changing rapidly as others "see the light". This will become more evident through 2011 as the consciousness changes and awareness shifts with the receptors opening to the

87

Divine light. The bodies change as more light enfolds. The abilities of healing open, senses expand, ability to sense and see energies opens. Communications, and telepathy all will begin to change into the new abilities. It may at times be confusing and troublesome but others will assist to help each to not fear this as it is natural that this evolution take place.

How this transition unfolds will be dependent upon the resistance created by those who choose not to yield to these powers and continue to suppress the vibrations. However it is not a question of whether this will occur, it is a question of how it will occur and how much drama is seeded and attracted back unto itself. The New Earth shift is unstoppable as it is the Divine Plan. How each chooses to align with this plan is a matter of free choice but all must heed the new Law of Infliction.

And so the big question: Do you want to stay behind and serve the gods or do you want to get a ticket to be God: Your Choice.

Looking forward on New Earth

The two worlds are transmuting in parallel. Now the old is overlain by new. The new is gaining its material substance while the old is losing its material substance. The energy of the beliefs of many—the one billion souls that have this knowing is increasing rapidly—has formed into a parallel universe. This is a different place built on a planet much like Earth as a start, like Genesis; but this time on the dreams and experience of higher vibration, where perfection is the normal, where love, harmony and peace are the cosmic rule. Here all the angels, ascended masters, archangels, and ascended cosmic beings walk and gather to teach and be part of that world. It is where manifestations and materialization are instant and discordant limitation cannot exist. What your mind can imagine can be.

This will puzzle many as to how it works but it is the purpose of the Time of Choosing and Revelation to become clearer to all as time unfolds and the new energy enfolds you. Perhaps you can think of it like when you sit down to make a plan to visit a place on vacation, or you want to create a summer home. As you congeal your thoughts into a plan, they form a hologram in your new world. Yes, once formed, they will be as real as your reality is now.

The players, the things, the consciousness are all set into a vast hologram which is formed by your collective. Yes, this can be modified as you learn to adapt to it. It is not much different than the way you now play in the 3D hologram of your 3D world but the difference is that most are not aware of how they are modifying it and manifesting their lives. But this is only a minor part of the infinite that can be explored and enjoyed, and created in this parallel Universe. As you proceed through the next year, it will become obvious how you can change this 3D one and it will help you understand the next one so you can become accustomed to how to manage in the new world.

As you learn this, you will be able to link across interdimensionally. Many are doing this now in an imaginary state. The pull and the ability to transcend the two in your existing form will get stronger as your vibrations lift to the next level. Now it is like a daydream that seems very real where you can visit or create things that your imagination and focus brings forward. You will begin to stay here where there is no time and you will comprehend how as you form your thoughts, they actually form into the hologram and remain. Yes, it will be something new to play with, will it not?

There is no discord here as it has been formed as your Heaven. It cannot support negative energies because they are of lower vibration. Similarly, although you will retain your bodies, or modify them, they will be of higher vibrational quality to be able to co-exist in this dimension. All the knowledge of the Universe will converge here through the guidance of what you already know and what they will teach. It will be a place that is a model of the Universe. You will be able to move between that Universe and this one at will.

Parallel to the formation of that 5D world that replaces your current 3D world, the light that has been emitted from you within, and the light that has been shining by the many requests of our service, is changing your world dramatically. The darkness will have no place and shadows cannot appear as the light shines everywhere. It is how the light of truth shines upon the dark deceptions and a new world is exposed. The truth about the financial system, banks, debt, about ETs, about religion, about Spirit, about big business, healing, politics, government, and their hidden agendas become visible.

The shock of this may be very high to many who resist the truth but at the same time, the same amount of light shines on many from outside and it is by choice and free will that they decide to add to the light from within. That is what many groups are here to assist with.

But, the 3D world as you see it now will continue and it will be up to humanity to determine how they evolve this world. What will be so different is that many will have evolved alternatives in cooperation with cosmic friends, and your own vast knowledge. But at the same time, as many of you begin to walk the planet as did Jesus the Christ, as you illustrate and show a better way, many will be led to a better way and eventually cross into the parallel world that you can tell them about the true heaven on Earth. For those who choose to ignore the light, will simply evolve in a personal and joint energy much as they do now, but in a way that provides them with healing, with faster manifestation and attraction—and they will become more aware of it. This may create many issues as their old values of religion and life come under severe scrutiny—and more and more turn to the light—simply because they will realize how they are creating things of their own choosing. On the other hand, through the Law of Infliction (discussed later), one can by choice create their own hell.

As each evolves and unfolds over the Time of Choosing and the current world shakes from the light upon it, many will learn to move between the dimensions at will. This will allow each to be here or there and even at the same time to teach and follow a parallel passion in this world. Many will still cling on to egoistic desires here and require much teaching and guidance. It is for the enlightened ones to teach how this is transcended—by example.

Know that upon acceptance you will phase into the new energy slowly. It will be like a dream, daydream, meditation, and then direct transfer by will. As your fuzzy outline grows, you will be able to see yourself phase shift in and out. When you go, you will go to that latest scene that you left from as it is simply suspended until your attention and awareness intersect that light. As you leave, the moment here will suspend itself awaiting your return. The hologram in your mind simply remains in virtual suspension, along with everything that is in it. All are suspended and as you quicken to this and realize your powers, you will change, rearrange, and materialize at will but only when vibration is above a threshold. At some point, the create stage becomes instant and your complete hologram can be changed as you would in a day dream where you can see or feel anything imaginable. This will take some time to get used to. At some point you will be able to show others this ability so you can lead others. It will be like making your own movies and entering them. These will initially be formed in a group consciousness place like your 3D Earth now but will change to allow whatever you imagine you want to be, or be part of.

By the changes occurring through the Time of Choosing as you further detach from old energy, the excitement will begin to turn inward as you look to Divine desires rather than 3D human ones. This is because ego is fading in its grip as you take on the trust and faith that you will create whatever you need to protect and nurture you. This is not a simple transition as you have been so trained to only have faith in yourself as an ego and trust no one. In this light it will be confusing to many and the old ways will not be released to the ways of faith and trust.

As you concentrate and learn your new senses they will awaken. Let the skill evolve naturally but always pay attention to their existence and their evolution. They will only become stronger if you acknowledge them and place your attention on them. You will begin to feel different—lighter, fuller, shinier, happier, more content, more confident in knowing the truth of us and yourself. Your sense will strengthen and be more united with us as we learn to communicate automatically. This is happening to many now.

Polarity, greed and conflict cannot exist anymore on New Earth than ice can exist in a world of fire. Certainly one can bring the ice into the fire, but it cannot remain in that lower state. Hatred cannot exist in a space filled with love and light. Disease and dis-ease cannot live here as well. This does not mean that it cannot change and that an ascended one cannot fall back but we see this as highly unlikely and not a model within the cosmos—certainly not one governed by God and not one where the individuals clearly understand they are creators.

Your new world will have the rules of the cosmos revealed and known. There are no mysteries and no hidden agendas. There are no reasons to want or fear.

Your Earths are holograms. How do they interact with you? Let us look at what you are familiar with—your movies which you can stack on a shelf. They are frames you call pictures, each one being a representation of an instant in time. They have no meaning or emotion to anyone until they are viewed frame after frame, now after now, each representing a replacement in your time of the other. By your viewing them in sequence, they present you with experience, emotion, feelings and even physical sensations. Yet they are nothing until you view them. Each movie sitting on the shelf has no time. Each frame sitting in your computer can be modified and changed, or the sequence rearranged at someone's will— even you if you created that movie.

So let us say you created many movies. One was done in Mexico near the ocean. One was done in the jungles of Africa. One was done in the desert. And one was done at home with family. So in your movies, you choose players. In the movies you have on the shelf these are actors and they can be in many movies at the same instant in time can they not. You and your players can be as well. Who you choose to place in your movies is up to you and they are in fact replicated if you want. Perhaps they are different characters but nevertheless the same person.

The place is the setting. It is your atomic world that appears real as the movie is created. Yet it is the same world on film. Each of the players is within that physical world. What if these worlds existed in parallel? And you were the producer who chose the actors and the settings? What if these segments or frames or "nows" were all sitting in a virtual space that your mind could access, string together, experience, or modify instantly by simply rearranging the frames or changing the pictures? Or perhaps rearranging the electrons into a new atomic configuration? What if you could simply suspend time by stopping the movie and entering a new one? The old one can be started from where it left off or it can be changed at will. And when you desire to view the other, you stop the new one and come back to the first.

This is similar to how a hologram is created and how you interact with it. At the level of higher vibration this is the way things are. It is natural and all commanded by conscious awareness. This is the way your different lives have been created and recorded as experience in your emotional body. They are all evolving at different rates or they have been played out. They are all "nows" in a virtual sea of experiences. And they can all be accessed, re-experienced, or even changed at will.

The mind can multitask in parallel and respond automatically. Many are already doing this at night. Most struggle with it in the day as they see no 3D representation or evidence of the work. It is happening, however, at its own pace as the body is not as quickly adjustable as the mind is. This means that over the next period, an adjustment in the sensory systems will change as the light being part begins to unfold.

This means that senses will change as sight begins to see energy outlines in other things. Hearing will expand to pick up subtle energy vibrations, the sense of knowing will improve. Many will begin to pick up thoughts, smell energies and sense them as being positive or negative, read other's energy being held for manifestation. The sense of feel and touch will expand as the invisible world begins to make more sense and it begins to overshadow the usual material world sensory system. This is the light body and the etheric energy of each duplicate that is now evolving from the heart to overshadow the 3D outer body. It is the next stage to evolving teleportation and telepathy and materialization like in the dream state.

It is a large transition and it is not an instant process in most. It will lead you into a new time space without limitations. It is beginning now.

And so there will need to be a decision as you have a taste of this during the Time of Choosing. It is one that requires the decision to serve gods on Old Earth, or be God on New Earth. It will be your choice.

6

RESURRECTION
THE TIME OF
TRANSFORMATION

The Time of Transformation

Once the choice has been made, the Ascension Train, and the process of transformation of Earth and humanity accelerates as the cosmic forces intensify. By choice and allowance through conscious intent the progression upon physical takes place as the train heads for New Earth.

The cosmic forces and energies, the photons, the planetary configurations and their relevant attributes, the solar and other rays act as transmitters to the receiving DNA antennae all together orchestrate the transformation. As they do the cumulative work upon the vessel of the body, it transforms and emerges. Through this period of Resurrection, the Earth itself changes and cosmic forces shift dramatically. And all life upon Earth that has chosen, or does not have a choice (like animal and plant life) also shift with it if in alignment. As Gaia shifts in vibration to purge old energies, so do those who choose to replace the old energies with the new, so the final transformation through unity and love can occur.

The vision of the New Earth—the hologram—is now born and it will be congealed from 5D through the total unity consciousness of love, to be overlain upon the higher ascended bodies of humanity and Gaia, which in turn chain reacts through the universe. To those who are not receptive, or do not board the Ascension Train, they will not be able to acclimatize to the New Earth higher vibrational energies and environment. They will find increased difficulty as the divergence between old and new 3D forms widen. Through the period of resurrection the process manifests above and below simultaneously faster and the differences become more dramatic.

The process of biological and mental shifting is being set in the 9th wave in humanity. The population upon the birth of New Earth will launch as the final transformation in preparation for the Great Alignment of Dec 21, 2012 and the final Solstice/Equinox. First the Cosmic Council of Planets and their astrological influences will attune into the etheric connection of each individual and the DNA antennae. It will be focused on each individual's physics as atoms and electrons open and increase as the space of pure love and more light pours into the quantum essence of truth and Unity of One.

Read into them will be the attributes and characteristics of their own essence the aspects of each frequency as it translates into the consciousness and then through to the physiology and chemistry affecting the thinking and behavior. It will be born and be drawn in a heightened outpouring of each of their essences, as will that which comes from the heart of God and the Central Sun of the galaxy. Acting as antennae each DNA molecule of the higher body will draw the information into local consciousness so that the attributes will evolve to greater functionality. Hence more metaphysical abilities will open to show to each and there will be as an insightful knowing of what is occurring. The development catalyst is intent and choice.

The Revelation is a result of the God and Christ Consciousnesses arising in all. When taken by choice, and when so taken it will begin to take prevalence and dominion over thinking. And by so doing this will wake up to the God Self and trigger body and chemistry changes each rising in the vibration of physicality through the infusion of light.

It means to receive and open to more light and the space between the quantum of love consciousness expands. This allows the body to become more interdimensional and nonlocal within the soup of love in all undefined space. The 3D and 5D aspects of energies first meld to 4D and then become One in all Dimensions. These are all wonderful Divine gifts that come from the opening of the truth within and the pouring of love from above; all triggering the opening of the DNA.

The higher abilities will begin to show as common to many of humanity. As each will come forward and many will move faster they will show others the way of this. Some are already able and the wave of showing will open from the knowing to be a force of consciousness upon all. This wave carries the understanding of the knowing of laws of manifestation and attraction. It will open to the working of it showing how the love unity consciousness has the engine of command available through the heart and the Divine mind.

The communications and the working of this following the 9th Wave will unfurl in great joy, overwhelming the 3D and 5D communication systems. The cosmic forces from the galactic center will be tuned higher and stronger as the DNA receptors engage and the body is acclimatized in steps. It is all thus readied for the information to be received and transmuted into the new reality of the New Earth and the New spiritually based Humanoid.

What will become more recognizable is the evolution of the human form as it will be seen by action of intent as the brightness and color of aura opens revealing the degree of light retained in the knowing. This will make it easy to identify and the knowing of struggle and darkness will be detectible as essence heightens in the body's shift in absorption of light.

Each will evolve at different rates and attain different levels of the DNA attributes. But most prevalent will be the sensing of others degree of love and light. Into 2012 this will intensify as the blue-white light is absorbed by intent of choosing and action of love and awareness in others. Otherwise it cannot be brought forward into the transmutation of cellular structure to crystalline-silicon form. As this grows stronger, the ability to receive will need to be in alignment with love energy or it cannot hold and the cells begin to pop their electrons into different atomic configuration of silicon base. This is through the DNA opening, the blue-white light, the cosmic forces, planetary energies, and the love from Source that all contribute. Then the reception vehicles of the body orchestrated by the heart and Divine mind play out their roles.

The body and material things will appear to be more translucent and the material world will feel softer, malleable and not as real as it fades in and out. This is so as the 3D and 5D aspects of energy signatures entrain into the temporary holding realm of 4D to be balanced, ready to meld upon each other's frequencies as One aspect of Unity. The consciousness of the Higher Self of the Divine Mind shifts into command to orchestrate this evolution of ascension and the knowing becomes shared and nonlocalized interdimensionally as the body begins to shift structure. The form will retain itself but all senses will expand, enhance in ranges and the body's abilities will widen in tolerance of temperature, sustenance, and acceptance to assimilate cosmic energies. All will greatly be enhanced in communications and knowing of elemental forces of Gaia and the cosmos.

The new Law of Infliction

Those not accepting of love and choosing of intent, in the later stages who have resisted, will not be able to receive the continued gifts and evolve in alignment with others the same way after the Time of Choosing. Although the consciousness will be filled with the knowing of the transformation, they can by choice of fear and resistance instigate their own demise. As this may be so, they may of their own free will leave by their own free will.

Alternatively they may learn to use the gift of instant manifestation in a positive way with pure intent (as it is not inflictable on others except in love and brotherhood) to live out their mortal lives in joy but still encapsulated with their own struggles as of their choice. Under the new Law of Infliction, no one will be able to inflict or affect others and this action will be known to them, and pointed out by others who will know and sense their difficulty. Those who choose to remain and act out their lives in Old Earth are not judged and will live their mortal lives out finding it more difficult to adjust to the shifting forms.

Those who do not choose to take the ticket will be left in the temporary 3D hologram overlain by the New Earth which will not be seen by them as they cannot see other dimensions now. New Earth and the new humanity which unfolds within it become the guardians and keepers of Old Earth. The new transformed ones will be free to walk both worlds if they desire to be of service. On Old Earth, much will be different for the transformation within the time of revelation affects all, and many who will choose to remain will still carry new abilities and capabilities, as well as being subject to limited shifts in physicality.

Of particular importance is the knowing of and the action of attraction and manifestation of experience. This is not of materialization and creation. They will also find several new abilities (if they accept them) as many had in the Old Earth and early days of ascension. And as physics shift this will create strain in adjustment of bodies. It is important here to know about the Law of Infliction which falls under the laws of attraction and manifestation. It states: ***Those who would inflict others with that which is not pure intent of unconditional love aligned with the Heart of Source creation, and who would act to impose this upon others without their knowing thus impose upon free will shall instantly by reflection bring upon themselves and their source the manifestation of such intent amplified one thousand fold, and instantly receive the knowing of this law***.

On Old Earth, this prevents anyone from harming another; and in such a way that the intent for harm is returned immediately to the one who so intends it. Of significance is that the knowing of this will prevail through the time of revelation. Should one desire to send love, this will be allowed at any time, but it will be of purity of purpose only—truly of heart and unconditional, not as dominion or avarice for ego will be immediately known for its selfishness. It does not destroy ego, it only reveals its intent. Infliction will take hold and those who remain in the Old Earth will live their lives as they prefer. The new changes will be difficult and there will still remain physical shifts, but at any time they can take the path of ascension as before under Old Earth. In such cases, knowing the power of manifestation in the positive side, ascension, even if remaining in old ways, can be dramatically accelerated, particularly with the service of those who learn to straddle both Earths.

It is this way because the cosmic and Divine gifts of ascension, the planetary alignments and the process of resurrection cannot be repeated, unless the Guardians of New Earth deem it so in unity. Then it can be poured out of the heavens once again to assist. The residents of Old Earth will therefore go through the usual life-death process as has always been, learning their way to ascension on their own free will as did Christ—the difficult way of lesson. At any time they will have the ability to depart, without judgment, in love to leave their 3D forms behind or to ascend in the old way in this old hologram as many before have done through tumultuous times.

Those who have chosen to ascend and have advanced rapidly may walk Old Earth to assist by teaching and be of service as was Christ for there will be many—as evolving crystalline light beings.

Thus during revelation all is revealed, no secrets, and no deception, all moved through the consciousness of New Earth. But it is important to know that those who stay may bring difficulty to themselves as will physical changes create difficulty. Others will know deception and struggle and these energies will multiply inward quickly onto them alone. God will not change the free will.

Then over time a new choice will occur in the shift from carbon to silicon forms. It occurs as light is absorbed and the ascension triggers activate the next metamorphosis. Gaia and Earth also parallel this process as she absorbs more light and activates the crystaline essence within an already silica dominant earth as they all ring and entrain together melding into the form of the New Earth.

So how do you choose? Will you continue on Old Earth to serve the gods, or will you take your ticket to New Earth and be God? Your Choice.

7

THE NEW EARTH GENESIS II-2012

The Virgin Birth of Christ Consciousness

Whichever way the bibles and the gospels paint the picture of Jesus Christ, and regardless of the many re-writes and underlying motivations to create a story for man's purposes, there is a common thread in all of it that cannot be denied. It is that this was a specially gifted human who had and showed unexplainable abilities. He allegedly walked this Earth showing these abilities particularly in the area of healing, was crucified for his teachings and abilities, and ascended after his death. Also, he was born of an unexplainable virgin birth, conceived through immaculate conception, or whatever anyone could conjure up as an explanation of some divine intervention. How these occurred and the details surrounding these events is where the vast writings come forward in confusion, variance and conflict. Over half the human population of planet Earth believe in some version of this as their truth. The same group also has some belief—in total contradiction of their scientific knowing that GENESIS I is a credible act of

"God". The many bibles and religious teachings do not deny this as they support *some* version of this story.

It is common that a Mother Mary was alleged to be responsible for the virgin birth of Jesus who became Jesus Christ, Son of God, or a Prophet according to Mohammed. But it really depends on who tells the story. Mother Mary was responsible for a conception and a physical birthing of the man who taught what he learned and showed special abilities very much beyond those of mortal men and totally misunderstood. Now, as new documents surface, new information about his teachings and his beliefs are coming forward. And these are totally contrary to the teachings that the bibles and gospels infer.

What is coming forward is he was a man of peace, believed in equality with women. He told his followers that they were all Sons and Daughters of God and that they could do exactly what he could show. All they had to do was find themselves as this power within was the power of love in the heart. Of course this would have been very difficult to do at that time of war, poverty and fear. Even before our End Times, to achieve this many would have had to sit as a monk on the mountain top for decades contemplating their navels. If you go back to the section on Christ Consciousness, this is what he reflected. That is why it is named Christ Consciousness. It is the part that rings truth.

Regardless, Mother Mary conceived and birthed this special man called Jesus who indirectly brought to humanity an epic legend that imbues the underlying belief in love, peace and goodness of all—the Christ Consciousness. She birthed a man who brought to Old Earth a consciousness that was to boil and evolve in humanity for two thousand years.

Now, in the year 2011 this same consciousness is being birthed into all of humanity at the same time that a New Earth is being conceived, again through Immaculate

Conception through the same one who incarnated as Mother Mary. It is Genesis II and it follows the process of "As above, so below" meaning it forms in the mind of God (above) as a Divine concept birthed through divine conception and born into reality (below).

Genesis II-2012

And so God looked at his creation and pondered it. He called his eldest Son P'Taah and his Daughter An'Ra forward as they were Co-Creators of Old Earth and they had born the one of Jesus Christ as Joseph and Mary. And he spoke:

"We have seen the evolution of the Old Earth and we have seen how all of your brothers and sisters have lived upon it. It has been a time when the spirit was allowed to be under dominion of the egos, and so it has been. Now we are seeing that humanity is bringing forward this spirit which we have quietly placed within them. It is a time to consider the New Genesis of New Earth that we shall conceive and give birth to. We see that birthing of Christ as agreed by you two and Sananda the one so incarnated has indeed left a legacy of spirit and that it has not been subjugated and it is still alive for all."

"It is a time that your brothers and sisters have earned their rights to know of themselves. This time we will allow the spirit to come forward in those that have chosen to know it and New Earth can be a perfect world that will be inhabited by the ones who so choose. In the beginning, it was as we had on Old Earth but it evolved away from spirit of true self to grow and know only unto itself. Let us once again create a new Genesis and allow the goodness of Old Earth to meld into the New Earth. This Genesis will be formed from the consciousness of those brothers and sisters that awaken, and we will so present them with the gift of ascension into the New Earth."

"But this time, Dear Ones, call forward your family of chosen ones and birth the new Genesis as the Divine feminine and the Divine masculine as the Kristos Consciousness. For as you have birthed through a Divine Conception your Brother of the one Sananda who agreed to birth upon Earth, so shall you give birth to the New Earth and all of the new humanity. For it has been that the masculine has been allowed dominion and it has served its purpose to create a new yearning for balance in all things. As you birth the New Earth through the new Genesis, so shall you imbed this consciousness of unconditional love upon all things."

"By the seeding on the equinox of March 21, 2011, it is thus that you will create the intent of conception of the New Earth. The time of seeding the birthing in Gaia's womb will be at a special place upon Earth that is familiar to you. It will be during the Time of Revelation, and it will be during the Time of Choosing. It will be within the 9th wave of Unity Consciousness evolution as this will be the time of gestation. The time of Dec 21, 2012 will bring the actual birth of the New Earth which will be as a new child. This will be a time like none other that will set the astrological imprint for the birth of New Earth. And so the time of Dec 21, 2012 onwards will be the maturing of the New Earth. The Time of Choosing will set the transformation platform for humanity. The time will be as a chrysalis shifting through 2012 up until the Venus transit. The final Grand Alignments will be when the emergence will become highly energized."

"By the seeding as with the immaculate conception, the New Earth will be the planting into the ethers of pure love family will have created the contract for the New Earth. It is here you will create the concept of form and purpose that will precede the conception which through the purity of Divine male and female will be conceived into creation. Here is the melding of the three elements; the pure New Earth as your creation of intent of pure consciousness as the melding of physical purity; the alignment of cosmic forces and planets; and the overlay

of the purity of love manifestation of Agartha, the new heaven upon New Earth. This is the process of conception as it is to be conceived as an egg of union of male and female upon the birthstone of a special location at a special time which you will choose, as you chose with the birth of Christ. In this, you An'Ra and you P'Taah will open the birthing lattice you require to overlay this upon the physical Gaia in preparation for the next stages, then you will seed this into that lattice to create Genesis II from above to below. It is as you have created Christ."

And so it is that a plan was made as we enter the last part of the End Times when the Kristos awakens to all Sons and Daughters of God. It is as we close out the cosmic cycle of 26,000 years. And so it is pre-ordained that this seeding is of New Earth and it will follow the process of the 9th wave into 4D which will include a 9 month gestation of the New Earth, beginning on the March 21 Solstice/Equinox and ending at the Dec 21st Solstice/Equinox shortly after the Time Of Choosing. It is the formation or congealing into 4D womb of the model of New Earth, ready to receive its inhabitants that have so chosen to evolve through the final stage of evolution to 3D. This is the plan for the new Genesis II that is conceived in the joint minds and is birthed as an egg of union of male and female as equal divine energies.

The birthing of New Earth

And so it was that under the guidance of Sananda, the one who walked as Christ, the time came to assemble the old family of souls upon Gaia in preparation for the new Genesis. And so it was that the ones of P'Taah and An'Ra who birthed Jesus 2011 years ago prepared for Genesis II. Twelve old souls gathered as the Crystal Council of Gaia as aspects of the Pleiadian Emissaries of Light. Over a year they had already prepared the groundwork for the birthing by realigning and reactivating the critical energy portals upon Earth and through the Galaxy. They had rejuvenated the old

Atlantian network through Tulum, Giza, Adams, Arkansas, and resurrected the Poseidon seed crystal, reconnecting all to the heart of Gaia and the heart of Source in the Galactic Centre. And so the family of An'Ra, P'Taah, KaTa Ra'An, Sa Yin Christas, Tata Naya Uwanat, Enoch, Eve of An' Ra, Te'Ra Nor, Ma 'At, Ayun, D`vina, and Awan Tu' Uwanat gathered upon the familiar sacred ground in Africa on the 21st of March, 2011 on the day of the Equinox.

Four were present in form and soul on the sacred site, eight souls were present in their aspects of frequency.

Within this sacred site sits the great black obelisk, an energy portal to the subterranean worlds of Agartha and Shamballa and the connection to Gaia's heart as well as her total essence as Mother Earth. At the time of the Equinox, it was known that a Star Gate would open so as to facilitate the birthing process of New Earth—Genesis II by those that had birthed Christ the same way. The process was as follows:

And Enoch said to the others: "*Let us join and ground ourselves in the NS—EW positions within the Obelisk. We will join hearts as the first internal pinwheel as Enoch, Te'Ra Nor, Ayun and D'vina. And as we join hearts we ground ourselves in absolute love. Now we call the second ring of P'Taah and An'Ra in the NW-SE position and Eve of An'Ra and Tata Naya Uwanat in the NE-SW positions. And now we call in the 3rd ring of Awan Tu' Uwanat, KaTa Ra'An, Sa Yin Christas, and Ma'At to join in a triple pinwheel of hearts*".

"*And now we connect all our hearts within the obelisk feeling the love as we connect to the heart of Gaia downwards and connect upwards to the Source heart of Creation so we are all one. Now we feel the flow of the obelisk, and the flow of energy from our hearts in absolute love within our pinwheel. Now I ask the crystal skulls to be brought forward as I ask Ayun to call them into position.*"

So Ayun spoke: *"We call forth on this momentous day the crystal skulls today of March 21, 2011. We feel the skulls hovering above our heads. Today we ask the melding of all of us here and all of planet and humanity to meld with the crystal skulls as we say this three times. And so we say crystal skulls, crystal skulls, crystal skulls. And so it is done."*

And Enoch said: *"Let us feel the essence come down through us."*

And Ayun spoke: *"I sense along with the skulls the Pleiadians who have been quiet are here. We have felt their presence for several days. They have done this to allow the essence of the crystal skulls to build to a centre point which we have now just achieved."*

"And now," spoke Enoch, *"I would invite those of our special Guides, Avatars, Archangels, Angels and Ascended Masters who have guided us to this point to join us. As well we invite those who are pure of heart to join us around the perimeter of this great circle. And we invite the Pleiadians as we invite those that wish to watch as we birth the New Earth. So we shall feel this energy, feel the connection down deep into Gaia and to source Creator as the heart of all that is and we feel the skulls vibrating, as we sense this iris of the Star Gate being completely open. We so project the aspects of An'Ra and P'Taah northward onto the ceremonial sacred place of the fertility stone so they may birth and bring forward the conception of the egg of the New Earth. And we ask P'Taah and An'Ra to open a special grid that is necessary for the fertilization of this egg. So they are now positioned upon the birth stone and this place."*

Te'Ra Nor spoke in Pleiadian: *"Ana watt ah hey ne nah. Ana watt ah hey ne nor An'Ra eh P'Taah. Ana ley a te how, Ana ley a te how, Ana ley a te how. Go in peace An'Ra and P'Taah, love to all, love to all, love to all."*

Then Enoch spoke: "*Now we take a moment of silence to allow An'Ra and P'Taah to bring forward the new grid and the New Earth. We see all connected to Gaia, Source Creator and to Gaia's heart. And so it is. And now as the iris of the Star Gate opens, it begins to spin clockwise and it connects upwards, up into Source, the center of the galaxy. And now it spins downwards as we drop down to hit the heart of Gaia as we pass through Agartha. And as we pass Agartha, we bring this model of heaven on Earth upwards so to be imprinted upon the egg, upon the birth of the New Earth and to be conceived as a model for all humanity to enjoy heaven upon earth. And so it is."*

"*And now I sense the crystal skulls will follow us as we drop through down to the other side of the Earth and as we are connected we all feel the heartbeat of Gaia as it becomes stronger and stronger. And with every breath and with every heartbeat she pours out her love upon all and allows the love to be brought in from all those within the universe that wish it to be so. With every heartbeat and every breath it pumps, pumps, pumps and we are so connected."*

"*And now with the assistance of the crystal skulls we join as one unit of Earth, of humanity, of all things, as one heart of the Creator and so we all completely enfold the planet with our love that is pumping through the heart of Gaia. Now with the assistance of the crystal skulls we connect the black obelisk with the rock to the north above the crystalline interface then to the two pyramids to the east and then north to the pyramid of Giza and the great crystal of Giza. We now connect the sapphire crystal of Tulum and the Arkansas green emerald heart crystal. And so they are all connected. And now we connect to the Easter Island heads and feel the connections as we with our hearts as one unit open the network and connect to the Great Temple of Poseidon and the great seed crystal. And now we feel the energies connecting across the planet to activate every pyramid, every portal, and as one heart we balance and align all these to create perfection in them to be as they were meant to be and meant to work. And so we are all surrounding the New Earth, Gaia and Old Earth as they will become One. We feel our heart energy and Gaia pumping love into the network and it reconnects and connects to all portals and chakras within the universe and it chain reacts through all dimensions and all worlds as Gaia is now the jewel of the universe again, her heart pumping with vigor to allow the ascension energies to flow and to move forward with grace and ease for all mankind and all things. Let us now feel the connection through the pyramids, through all dimensions and feel the spinning vortexes up and down, through the heart of Gaia and all that is the universe."*

"Now we bring back P'Taah and An'Ra into the center of the circle. They have completed their birth and join us. We ask the skulls to do what they mean to do, raising the consciousness of the entire planet and to bring forth the knowledge and the knowing they carry. And so it is dispersed within the grid and the pyramids and the energy portals and the crystal through Poseidon now all connected to Gaia. And now is there anything to be said, if so say it now."

So Ayun spoke: *"The Pleiadians welcome you all, all earthlings to the new energy. It will build in the years ahead. We hug you as we do other ET beings here. Today is the time of great joy and great love. And we feel our hearts melding. Welcome."*

Enoch spoke: *"As we feel this great energy of love and unity consciousness, it is our knowing that the crystal skulls have revealed what they are required to reveal at this time. It is to know that this ascension and the bringing forth of New Earth conceived so will enfold for all today as done upon this egg. Conceived with the egg we have visions of the Council that they wish to declare this day to be seeded into the grid, Gaia as declared by the council. We as creators do seed into the process of*

111

birth the following energies as declarations from our hearts as One".

"And as Creators, we of the Council do seed into the process of birth of the New Earth these energies by our declarations from the heart: And so we declare from our hearts that the consciousness of the planet will shift to the total awareness of the power of Divine love, to the cosmic laws of the One, so there will be no strife nor disease upon the land. And all that were, became sovereign of spirit and found their ways Home to bring Heaven upon themselves and hence the New Earth, knowing that we are all One."

And Ayun declared: "And so we declare from our hearts that a new energy of monetary exchange will be born and there will be no lack and no need. And within this the new energy of banking institutions of sovereignty will be birthed so there will be only abundance and prosperity enfolded with honesty, love, and integrity of the heart. And all that was the old energies of debt is forgiven and the true worth of sovereignty and monetary energy will abound in all of humanity. And nations and people will be set free to live in harmony and abundance."

And Te'Ra Nor declared: "And so we declare from our hearts that the awareness of the Earth Dweller's cosmic neighbors will open and the skies will be filled with jubilation of peace and harmony in the bringing of the New Earth into the Intergalactic Federation of Planets and Star Nations. And the new technologies of the Universe, in harmony and Divine Love, will flow and blossom in the fulfillment of the One. And the Pleiadians, the true ancestors of mankind, will come forth in celebration and love to join as brothers and sisters with their true family."

And D'vina declared: "*And so we declare from our hearts that boundless free energy will appear everywhere, with special projects to replace old through an easy and peaceful transition to that which is in harmony with Gaia. And the planet will flourish and blossom again as the true laws of Nature reveal themselves to humanity. And the rising of the Great Crystals and cosmic laws of the Golden Age of Atlantis and Lemuria will be brought forward in the true essence of all in a magical kingdom of Heaven of Agartha as it is enfolded upon the New Earth.*"

And Enoch declared: "*And so we declare from our hearts that Gaia is fully healed, balanced and reborn as New Earth so her position within her cosmic body will be perfection again. And the New Earth will be born into the Source energy of love and perfection so Gaia will abound in the glory of her essence, shining as a jewel in the Cosmos, radiant and glimmering with divine love infusing her being and all that is upon her. And as the Atlanteans and Lemurians rise again through the crystal skulls, she will heal her being and enfold her wondrous offerings to the Cosmos and all life forms, to reveal to all of heart the true crystalline essence of nature's secrets and the wonders of the Universe.*"

And Ayun declared: "*And so we declare from our hearts that mankind will choose to fully awaken to its Divine heritage. And it will be that their DNA and Chakra systems open to their fullest functionality, open all the attributes of the God Self, Divinity, and the higher powers of Creator and the Heart. And the new human will walk in lower forms upon Gaia in full divine consciousness, as an eternal being of Light and Love, omnipresent and multidimensional totally knowing and One with all that is, was and will be.*"

And Enoch declared in Pleiadian: *"And so we declare as a Council that it be so, and it is so done. At ta natiah lah nah tia lah eta nah eta lah na ate dad ah low ate nah nah tah tita als wanta so too wah."*

And Ayun spoke*: "Ah he ah na nah ya hool ya nat tah wah hee na nah ta hal la tah hah.*

And Enoch spoke: *"So let us feel the energy, feel the sense of completion and allow the skulls to do their melding of their work and to allow the Divine minds that we have all given command to unfold what is to unfold and what our true paths are. And so it is in love and of the heart. We all speak as One."*

And Ayun spoke*: As One. The universe is cheering. The Earth is applauding. Everything that we envisioned has come to pass."*

And so the second Genesis II was born.

A glimpse of heaven on New Earth

The New Earth is an unfolding of heaven upon Old Earth. The process by which this unfolds after Dec 21, 2012 will be similar to a process of frequency entrainment. The holograms of Old Earth of 3D meld into the hologram of New Earth that originates in the Consciousness in 5D. Although this process may seem beyond comprehension now, this will become more apparent by that time. In the process of this melding, New Earth is in 4D, awaiting the shift of Old Earth into the same dimension.

In mythical writings, something that has stuck like glue through all time, are the stories of Shambala, Agartha, Hyperborea, there are many. These have been places of subterranean worlds that represent the perfect world of Heaven. Even upon Earth itself are the times such as the Golden Ages of Lemuria and Atlantis that once were based in times of unity, perfection and the love of one; highly spiritual in the civilization's essence.

One aspect they have in common, whether myth, fact or fiction, is that they reflect a gnawing preoccupation for a better place to live, and a place that is tuned into the more spiritual aspects of humanity. It is like the relentless quest for the Divine Self.

Such is the place called New Earth. It is a place that has been formed by the Unity Consciousness where all is one and everybody and everything knows it. There are no egos or lower vibrational energies. It is a place formed by the great creative energy of the cosmos—unconditional love—where the true form of Light Being can be separate from the lower form without having to die. Yes, a place of ascension that is Home—where the real You came from as a segment of the total consciousness of the Creator, or God, or whatever you want to call it. And the real You created this place in combination with other real Yous as the place of permanent residence.

Here all things grow and expand and experience in the soup of love, that which is all that exists. Here anything can be created instantly in a personal hologram that is shared with others. In this respect if you think about those 100 trillion molecules of DNA (discussed later) that all instantly link together in quantum love and operate as one, consider your true being and its hologram as one of nonlocal trillion holograms that are acting as one.

Here you can create and relate to anything in a lower form as you have overcome the lower vibrational draw of ego and separation to know who and what you are. This is what ascension is all about. Thus in this place everything lives in a higher vibration and those lower vibrations like fear, struggle, conflict, deception—those things that are not true of heart and with the pure intent of unconditional love—simple cannot be. It is like ice cannot exist in steam, a higher level of vibration.

115

Here in this world, anything imaginable is possible. The free form of Light Body, universal to all, is free to meld, to move into, or out of any other form with their agreement. Here you can create your own form as you can your environment—instantly. It is a place that allows other beings and other worlds to have their own model of this perfection. Here constructs can be created instantly, as can anything imagined that is in harmony with the environment and all that exists there. Everything is telepathic. All forces of 3D such as gravity that acts upon non-quantum particles is overcome. It is thus all governed by Divine laws of One and commanded by the Higher Divine mind which is part of the One Mind. The big constraint is that it is in total absolute alignment with the soup of Creation and the Mind of Creator—unconditional love. For that is where the true power of creation resides.

It is like now that you can do this in the hologram of a day dream. Time ceases and all is eternal, yet when life is given, it lives, grows and experiences in accordance with its Divine design of its DNA. This hologram cannot be imagined yet, and a 3D linear mind trapped in the 3D form of human cannot yet comprehend this. But this hologram of Earth is of this nature and this will become more understandable and the truth known as the Time of Choosing unfolds.

New Earth is such a hologram where the conscious desire of the many forms the New Earth with the heaven overlay. As time progresses, the Old Earth will meld with this New Earth.

The melding of Old Earth and New Earth

The melding of the two Earths will occur after 2012 in 2013 as the lowered form entrains and rises in vibration and all upon it do as well. It rises to meet a higher, stronger vibration awaiting as New Earth in 4D.

Understand this is not an event but a process of evolution of consciousness above translating as an overlay onto the action of transformation below. It is as when one or masses decide to act and change the physical engagements and physicality of environment below. The transformation occurs as from consciousness above in 4 and 5D to lower form and into 3D and lower forms. As this ends after 2012 it is lifted to a higher vibrational status.

The physical process is similar to the stages occurring as the DNA and chakra system work in unity of opening the coding programmed in DNA. To be executed by the chakras into physicality and chemistry of cellular structure as initiated by DNA, intent and triggers from cosmic impulses act to combine and transform. As bodies shift into higher vibration and form, they will sense and feel differently as the DNA blueprint opens to the layers and the chakras open to their full abilities in conjunction with the cellular modifications of upgrade. This will be difficult for many who have not chosen when physical changes are not occurring to acclimatize into the new vibration. It creates mental and physical dysfunction much like the alleged dysfunctions of the Crystal Children—which are not dysfunctions at all—they are characteristics of a higher vibration not coping with the old vibration. There will be many to assist in this.

There are millions now upon earth that already exhibit the first stages of the transformation. They can sense discord and they can heal the energies. It is as Christ walked, and there are thousands coming forward like the example of Sai Baba who can materialize objects and shift interdimensionally. These are the ways of Christ who came to demonstrate and to imbed the spirit of the Christ Consciousness as a birthing process that has lasted 2000 years in preparation for the final birthing.

An example of two new aspects that are occurring now are healing and energy sensing. There are specific stages that will become common for millions upon millions as they exhibit the abilities of Christ and walk as he did. Stage 1 is to heal a perception of discord, it is simply done in the mind. Stage 2 is to heal a physical discord by 3D action originating in consciousness. Stage 3 is to heal via an energy balancing from the heart. Stage 4 is to connect the divinity of heart and create the instant miracle of healing. Stage 5 is to create as a Creator directly transmuting materials or creating material from the substance of love. There are hundreds of other new attributes and abilities encoded within your DNA that will evolve the same way.

The ability to walk this way in all stages upon Old Earth is opening to millions. This *is* the Christ Consciousness rising after 2000 years of gestation in preparation for the New Earth Genesis. This time however, the consciousness is rising as the Kristos Consciousness. It is the balanced Divine male and Divine female, for the masculine energy has had its time of dominion for 2000 years. Its purpose was to teach what is not needed upon New Earth. As the evolution accelerates through Stage 4 and 5 to dominate unfolding as the Consciousness of Kristos, this will prevail upon all minds and all things. And thus all that is can be healed of discomforts even if some prefer the struggle of Old Earth. The environment and all Earth will over time transform into the perfection of balance and root in the unconditional love of the heart. It is only that which is perfection that exists on New Earth. As the Kristos Consciousness evolves to be expressed by millions attaining Stage 5, instant miracle healing and materializing become a norm as Creators take their rightful roles.

The personal transformation

Imagine one day that you go to a movie theatre and watch a show. You are captured by the show that is playing out before your eyes and you feel emotions that grip your heart as you engage in the story of a family that has had much grief. The story moves you between the joy and the sadness as the patchwork of drama lifts and affects you. Afterwards, you sit with your friends and you discuss this. You feel that it was very interesting and that it captivated you and you can relate to the drama but you have a tendency to take a higher perspective of how you would play it out much differently. Yes, if it was me, you say, I would have done it differently.

Now, you go home and go to sleep. What if that morning you suddenly are sitting 15 feet above the bed in a nice cloud-like chair. There below you see you beginning to awaken from the sleep. You observe how you awaken slowly and watch with great interest as this physical you goes about the business of the day. You watch as you sit with your wife and begin to talk about this movie again. They are discussing how the death of the child was such a trauma and how it devastated the father to the point of total annihilation of reality. As You listen, You begin to hear what you is saying about how you would have reacted much differently. But You, from a higher perspective think no, that is not in your constitution. That you would not react that way and you would also have great trauma in dealing with it. From a higher perspective, however, you feel it was a lesson, but not to dwell on it until you lose that which is dear to you—your life and sense of value.

Now think about this because one day soon this is exactly what you will see. You will realize that this hologram of Old Earth is just like that movie in the theatre. Now let us suppose that You decided that you must bring this higher perspective down into that lower life movie where you are busily deluding yourself. So suppose you drop down into the body and now you begin to speak a different way from a much higher perspective—and your Higher Self. Then you went back up after. Think about this because this is what you are trying to do but your Higher Self has been blocked.

Changes in the next years for so many will be spectacular. As some evolve to show special new characteristics, these will lead others by example, as did Christ. As they watch they will see how all can grow, heal, become telepathic, co-create and will show what a vibration at a higher level means. Bodies will become fuzzier as each begin to shift between the dimensions. The forms will eventually become different from those that stay but each new form will be able to be in both dimensions. Most important is that the holograms and how they work will become clearer to an internal "knowing".

So… What is it you will choose? To remain serving the gods or to be God? Your Choice.

8

WHAT ARE YOU?

As a recap, the specific Divine Plan has been to allow Gaia and Mother Earth to ascend at this special time. But the overall Divine Plan is and always was to allow all that is to ascend so as to bring the aspect of the God Self to lower form to experience and to expand the joy of its wonder. At this point it is the time of Gaia's and Earth's ascension that is to be completed with the alignment of galactic center—her origins. She and Earth have offered themselves in sacrifice to be the body and form of the Great Experiment of souls to bring all things upon her and be connected to her in the ultimate evolution of spirit. It is her destiny.

The Divine Plan has been for humanity to be allowed to ascend with her by their own free will—God's gift to all should their worthiness to ascend show when they recognize the power of love as the ultimate power and truth. It is the Divine Plan to find self as hidden within all equally, the knowing of the God Self. Here the attributes of Creator and Creation await a time to be as one, in all equally, and awaken this as a spark of quest of self and Home as accessed through the heart, the seat and power of the Divine self. And so this is encoded within the DNA, placed within each, in a place where it could never be lost, within each heart, to find the way to its truth, and to bring it forward into consciousness. It is the Divine Plan to allow each and all to grow, evolve and express the joy of love and to receive love and bliss in return so as to ascend in form and to make greater and expand the totality of love of the Creator as the supreme force of all that is. It is the Divine Plan to allow all possibilities in all beings equally and allow by free will that which they desire first in the thought above, then to form below as their ascension evolution. The Divine Plan is to allow creation with the tools of love through the gateway of the heart. And as humanity has shown its worthiness in love, so it is that the Divine Plan is now manifesting upon Gaia and Earth, into new form in wondrous expansion of the universe which is God's mind.

Truth is the catalyst to change

Well, you say, that's a great plan but that's a whole lotta' changes in a short while; especially when you look at the state of Earth now. So think upon a situation that may be closer to your comprehension. Think about how the overall consciousness about the "truth" in the stock market can change lives instantly. Suddenly a shift occurs; one of withdrawal from a belief that the market is going up forever, or some danger lurks. What happens? What about a 40-50 percent drop over a week? It drops as people start grabbing profits or getting out. Does this change a lot of balance sheets fast? And a lot of lives? It happens when there is a withdrawal of support from a previous belief. It is like a marketing tsunami that shifts minds instantly. The drama occurs because so many begin to think the same thing at the same time and they take physical action from a shift in conscious belief. Then another wave of panic ensues created by the first, and so it happens—in a matter of months. The reason for this is that there has been a huge underlying current of consciousness shifting to fear

122

of loss that creates a feeling that something is "amiss" and danger lurks. And then a flash point occurs and bingo!

So what happens when the truth of religions hits the mass consciousness? What about the banking system? About the Federal Reserve hoax? About our political leaders? About the medical system and drugs? About the corporate monsters who feed people marketing crap? About the Vatican mafia? People already have that feeling like Neo of the Matrix had; that something is not right about these gods and self proclaimed Gods of commerce and religion. People have placed their faith and trust in a story that is a contrived construct for some purpose that may not be so ethical. What of this part truth-part lies story of Christ and the birth of Earth?

Have you noticed the shift that perhaps the powers that be have been pushing a load of BS into everybody's minds? So everyone is ripe just like in the stock market. So what is the catalyst for the shift? Truth.

So far the truth of Christ and Creation has been withheld, as has the truth about your Divine powers— just like the truth of the stocks in the example having no real value. The truth that Christ had a whole different philosophy and was a simple man like you and I that believed what he was and developed all these ascension abilities (the hard way I have to say) before his time has been hidden. And then there is a fantastic myth about all us sinners (especially the women) that has been perpetrated into the consciousness of the Old Earth, ready for correction. Sinners? Really? It would seem it is the perpetrators that may be the sinners. What if that is the real truth?

But there are two things that are very important about this religious deception. First, it has kept the mass of humanity conscious about Christ. It's the wrong story but that's ok because it is the consciousness of the many that has clung onto the real truth and is ripe for a shift.

Secondly, there is an underlying wave of the right story now as there are huge numbers of people moving into this consciousness. Also, there have always been many esoteric foundations particularly in eastern cultures that do support the right process of love, peace, and the power residing in what is described as your Higher Self. They are just waiting to say: "*I told you so*".

And so you may be wondering at this point of the tale how it is that this new yarn of the Ascension Train can take place. How is it possible that Revelation and Resurrection can unfold in such a short time? It is because the other part of you that was relegated to the back seat of the car is taking command and it is not your human body with your limited mind of intellect and ego. It is ego that is now headed for the back seat. It is because underneath a new belief tsunami and this new energy developing is releasing your true counterpart. And it is because many are already looking for the escape path from what does not feel quite right. That paves the way to a fast move.

So who is the new driver? What is this counterpart? You may be wondering what you are if not a human body. Let us go into this space. Remember that the whole key here is consciousness and intent. It is the catalyst in the quantum world where anything is possible, and it can shift fast. Without it, like it is known in quantum physics, nothing happens. When this occurs at this time in mass, things will happen—fast. It is noted that this process of ascension—that which many have achieved before—has traditionally not been so simple as one had to dedicate their whole lives to the inner processes whereby it was achieved. That is not the case in this time. In effect you have to do nothing this time except believe and allow.

Overlaying your mortal body which we refer to as 3D, is a life force made up of invisible magnetic systems. The expanding body of belief refer to this being as a Higher Self in 4D, 5D, and higher D's. When they leave, like in a Near Death Experience, the overlay goes on a little vacation, and if you are lucky, it may come back to wake up the 3D body again. If not, then in simple terms, the 3D body dies and the Light Body goes "Home".

The easiest way to describe this is a Light Body which in simplest of terms is like your aura that includes DNA, the physical quantum body and the chakra system that are like the receptors and transmitters between physical and non physical. The thing that holds this all together to keep it going is the mind—consciousness. Part of it is to manage the lower form of 3D, instinct, ego, (Lower Self) the other is to manage the higher form of your divinity (Higher Self). Over 90% of this is quantum space of "no thing" or to scientists "nothing". If you are a quantum physicist then you will relate to this. Well, to those shifting into higher vibration these days this "nothing" is quantum love.

Your quantum biology

Your DNA is 90% mostly quantum which is why mortal men and their narrow science can't see it or observe it. It is only partly biology as it overlays and interfaces to create a link with a physical biology as your lower form of sensing apparatus. Accept for now that quantum is what love is in its primal substance of creation in a form of waves, frequencies that constitute the mind of God—Total Consciousness. No one can really define love or consciousness in 3D terms of science, so this description here should not be hard to accept for the moment.

To understand quantum look at your individual mind. As you close your eyes, place your attention on an image of an object. It forms from the fabric of love as an image representation coming instantly into your awareness. What is it? It is a representation of a physical form created by your attention of it in your mind. That process is called the Observer Effect in quantum physics that perplexes scientists. Now see another object the same on the other side of the planet. Objects, or coherent frequency aspects representing something, have no regard for time, space, and are formed anywhere instantly.

They are all interconnected as one instantly and can be anywhere as they are all within the same soup of love, formed from the same essence of consciousness. These are all aspects of simple frequencies that the mind creates by attention and intention to that which is familiar. It is nonlocal—can be everywhere, nowhere. It formed instantly. This is another term that science struggles with. Now what of another term of collapsing the wave? Science knows this as collapsing from the wave state of primal soup to the atomic state of supposed 3D form. In so doing you bring an image into manifestation into 3D—such as a healing miracle—where suddenly the atomic state is re-arranged into a different healed state.

And should you project such images from the heart, and from the 3rd eye, one reflected back from Source to intersect the other, you form the hologram of existence from the primal soup of love by way of the mind. It, in quantum lingo is entanglement and is simply a shift in frequency, a rearrangement of the soup through the mind and the use of intention.

Both the mind and DNA are quantum as are the chakras, all quantum energy is awaiting intention to shift form into any possibility imaginable—as with the object we began with. And what is the vehicle that instigates the shift into material form? The heart and the torroids aligned on the chakras, all simply formed from invisible divine energy.

And what are you? A quantum light being interfaced to a 3D biology through DNA and chakras which interface to chemistry and biology through cosmic intelligence and your own intent that drives it. It all takes instruction from the mind and intent. And it is done in pure love, aligned with the sea of love, so you are one with all of it, in the same quantum realm where all possibilities exist, waiting to be formed by intent, so everything can be created, and sensed as experiences. Life manifested by the simple act of conscious intent—as with the example of the object. It is because you are one with the sea of love and all that is, all that you are as quantum biology, open to your higher aspects of divinity through the lower aspects of form. Why? Because you intended to be so and you already are so and by the alignment, you make it so once again. Your natural state. It is the same as the Observer effect in the 3D hologram in which you live, for it is no different than the 3D hologram that you formed with the objects—all in the mind of consciousness—that which science cannot explain.

Your quantum DNA

First, let us look at this DNA and in this section I basically bring forward the work of Kryon, the foremost world "expert" in this "esoteric" area. In the DNA of all humans are 12 double strands that include Divine Consciousness. Thus this DNA that we all carry represents pieces and parts of the God Self and the Higher Self. The Human body is one of the only places within all life forms that has this quantum atomic structure—the only one which you will find in a 3D existence. It has a quantum overlay of the complexity of 3 billion parts and only 3% (protein encoded parts) is in a seeable dimensionality. DNA is a single source of 100 trillion pieces of chemistry all singing the same song. Nothing else in the body does that and it is identical throughout the body.

There is an awareness of DNA eight meters around you called Merkabah which is a Divine field, a multidimensional mist created by the DNA event, a hundred trillion pieces working as one. The field contains all that is your DNA. At birth the field is at 30% brightness. Ascended masters are at 100%. It is like a single atom that has a space filled with patterning that cannot be seen because DNA is a multidimensional spiritual event.

With awareness comes activation of DNA. Humans can only address the entire DNA field, not a specific layer. The truth is you activate it as an innate aware system of DNA as it knows what you are trying to do. It will decide what layer to activate and when, not you. The activation is in the intent and the awareness so for example the healers are not addressing specific layers or areas. It is the DNA mist that will decide waiting to communicate to a cellular level. All DNA has a mini magnetic field.

Together the DNA molecule fields overlap to create a sonority of love. This creation is in you. It is important to visualize this to open communications of what you want to work on as DNA does the rest. DNA is completely multidimensional, interactive with itself; nothing ever does the same thing. It is quantum energy that shifts depending on what it needs. There is no time, place or when or where anything is. All is everywhere together, all is one. For it to work, 100 trillion parts must know something at the same time and all pieces must agree through an energy absorption of consciousness in a 3D construct within your reality (you called it a process of photons called entanglement). DNA is identical everywhere over the body, but specifically and uniquely yours.

Trillions of copies talk to each other instantly or you could not exist—it is a process of communications between DNA loops—quantumness within a soup of magnetics. Each DNA has a magnetic loop that has a field overlapping to the loop next to it. Trillions of loops equals one consciousness—a magnetic imprint you carry. Magnetics is an interdimensional quantum energy and this as an imprint creates the human aura which is not a magnetic field. It is a result of the confluence of DNA communications within the body—quantum imprint—melding of energy to create a quantum field not measurable.

In the current Time of Choosing, five layers are affected in this shift and these are always affecting each other. It is being opened without you even knowing. Nothing will happen as a result if you don't want it to. It will continue to be enhanced but remain dormant. This is why the intent of the Train Ticket is so important. Without intent in quantum nothing happens as conscious awareness is the catalyst and driving force, just like the example in the stock market. The energy of the planet talks to your DNA through the magnetic field of what is love.

Those being affected now, in the Time of Choosing, the Revelation are Layer 2 which is Life Lesson. It links to layers 7 and 8. It is not karma in its purpose. *"I do not ever want to be alone"* equals a life lesson to be alone, what you have not yet accomplished in your life lesson and will continue until learned. But now it is altered. Layer 6 is Higher Self and now you have access to it. Layers 7 and 8 are married as the creation layers of Akashic. The first gift is the ability to have spiritual wisdom to know your purpose, your lesson, feel love, and connecting. If you go to meditation and say *"I would like to pull upon a lifetime when I could..."* to draw a talent through intent—it will pull and this will develop and evolve at its own pace. Layer 9 is the Healing Layer—it heals Akashic. You heal yourself by healing Akashic *"I want to inform my DNA I am a Master"*. That is what regression and psychology is all about—to find the cause in history and to change the perception/belief. The Higher Self will go back and bring this out from Akashic. You are asking for information only, that's all that's there. These are your current gifts. In your meditation push on these with the light of pure intent.

But... if you care not, or believe not, and follow the same old crappy ways of the blue pill, consciousness is void of new intent, and... yes the same old crap.

DNA is the core element of who you are physical and spiritual and the Higher Self dwells here, along with past lives, and karma—all is here in quantum parts. Each molecule of DNA is 3 billion chemicals strong, each loop so small you need a microscope. Only 3% of DNA chemistry does anything—the protein encoded portion which produces thousands of human genes. It is the blueprint of life with 90% of DNA a quantum blueprint of your divinity. Within the 90% is human consciousness—the way you talk to DNA.

DNA is the core block with four groups or bases. Its sequence of bases makes the genetic code in a double helix of pairs twisted in a spiral code as 3 billion base pairs long occurring 100 trillion times. The code has 23,000 genes of who we are. A gene is a hereditary unit in a living organism. This is the double helix molecule in a chemical system representing those 3 billion parts. The **DNA Event** is the sacred core of life, the love of God mixed with dimensional confluences and the joy of creation.

In each DNA molecule there is a mini portal to a multidimensional Universe. Humans know who they are and even plants and animals know this but one must first become aware. This may be difficult to believe, but when birth occurs, there are five key elements imbued in DNA:

1. Hereditary of parents biology

2. Karmic imprint
3. Astrological imprint as determined by magnetic pattern through inductance from sun
4. Akashic record
5. Sacredness of God

The DNA Layers

According to Kryon, there are 12 double strands of DNA, which since 100,000 years ago was seeded into humankind by the Pleiadians as the first time it contained the aspect of Divine Consciousness. Earth became the first planet of this seed which had the choice of Free Will to accept their Divine roles as creators or not. Kryon states: *"DNA is a process of love, more than chemistry, an event defining the core of sacred life, the love of God within the Universe, mixed with dimensional confluences and the joy of creation. DNA is the crossroads of God and man, the mixture of quantum and non-quantum attributes with the essence of the truth of the Universe."*

Well, let us see what it is you are missing. Within these 12 Layers, there are four groups:

GROUP 1: GROUNDING
LAYER 1 is the **Biological layer**. It resides firmly in 3D and is multidimensional—the one we see. It reacts to the other layers. It facilitates communication directed by human intent. 3% is biology, the rest is a multidimensional soup that directs the biology energies into action—miracles. It is the double helix and represents the chemistry you can see.

LAYER 2 is the **Life Lesson** partner to Layer 8. It is the default guide for direction as unfinished business. Karma was dropped in 1987 through Harmonic Convergence.

131

LAYER 3 is the **Ascension and Activation** layer. Every Master who walked the Earth was biological and was legendary had 100% active DNA (we are at 30%). Ascension is moving to the next lifetime without dying. Thousands have done this, voiding karma, balanced duality, worked on their life lesson to become someone else. The process is directed through layer 3. Activation means connect something into reactive form. So the layer is about Masters and is the action layer that directs the chemistry of your body to the double helix to create something that is not active into something that is.

GROUP 2: HUMAN DIVINE
LAYERS 4 and 5 are the **Angelic Name** Layers. As you birth on the planet you split into parts as you cannot exist on Earth in your full God form. You are part of a quantum soul group. The largest part of the split is Higher Self that separates in a quantum way, into the DNA not in 3D. The next split is what you call Guides and Angels, yours for life. They are parts of your own soul group. When you shift vibration, the guides back away to allow you to adjust and settle in. They do the same then rejoin later. They are you and then when settled, you can communicate better. During this time there is loneliness and no purpose as DNA adjusts its vibration. The third group is the soul group as an entourage of you, as trillions of soul pieces who work together to support humanity along with the ones on the other side of the veil waiting to be structured by your intent—the most powerful force on the planet. When you co-create you do it with all soul groups to facilitate what is best for all. So what you do for yourself drives what is good for the planet as it drives the vibrational engine. The time is chosen on its own schedule, not to your own schedule as this is a sacred process. As a piece of God, you have an angelic name. So as you see the whole you recognize a piece of you—that is the quantumness of the family

within you. This name is your label in the cave of creation in your individual soul crystal, a record of all soul groups from each Higher Self, part of the Gaia energy library kept there forever. Layer 4 and 5 are ether Light and the power of the core crystal energy. This is the essence of your expression all your divinity on the planet, the name on the crystal of the Akashic record.

LAYER 6 is **Higher Self Prayer and Communications**. This is the brother-sister that is absolute divinity. When Masters walked before they were mocked and killed. This time it will be bigger, all together. DNA is the vehicle to something else, not the end in itself, beyond what you can imagine—to the Higher Self. Talk to DNA and give any direction (you don't care when you are in charge how or what is said as to a right or wrong way). DNA waits for instruction. The Higher Self is the door to divinity. It is a pathway and manifestation portal through prayer and meditation. This is the I am layer that is the portal for communications to God, the frequency of the Creator. Layer 6 works with layer 3 to produce layer 9— completion.

GROUP 3: LEMURIAN
This group belongs to the Lemurians, not Pleiadian origin.

LAYER 7 **is Divine Revelation** layer, the end of the innocence and the beginning of spiritual awareness. This is one of 3 Lemurian layers given to humanity 100,000 years ago.

LAYER 8 is **Master Akashic** records, past lives, and karmic record. The energy of all that exists is who you are today is here.

LAYER 9 is the **Healing** layer and works with Layer 1 to heal. It responds to human consciousness through prayer, meditation, worship, faith, positive thinking, such as in healing miracles. It is the second immune system and does nothing unless you talk to it and it does not abide by chemistry rules as in Layer 1. Lemurians knew this. Their rejuvenation temples were not machines but consciousness resonators. The St Germain violet flame is a direct use of Layer 9. For example, there are four modes of healing: Allopathic is a cause and effect chemical process (3D medicine, drugs). Homeopathic creates signals for chemical change like acupuncture. Next is Energy Work 1 that addresses the Merkabah to balance it, and Energy Work 2 directly addresses the DNA at the core level through human consciousness.

GROUP 4: DIVINE GOD
This is all quantum meaning it is Interdimensional and everywhere at once, all interlinked as one.

LAYER 10 is **Divine Source** and belief, a call to understand your divinity—the human search for God. Humans must ask for it, and recognize it.

LAYER 11 is the **Wisdom of Divine Feminine** of pure compassion and mother energy. The Venus transit of 2004 activated this slightly, the next final activation is June 2012.

LAYER 12: is **Almighty God**. It is a part entangled in you as this is the only planet this Almighty God creator energy exists in its creations. It is powerful beyond belief if you deploy the wisdom of love and integrate it with the divine feminine. Layer 12 works with 3 the Ascension Layer.

It is noteworthy here to bring forward something that Kryon says (and is enforced by just about everyone on this enormous bandwidth). Many not of the Light have learned to capture this energy through fear which immobilizes DNA to shut down all but survival instincts. It's those blue pills again!

The bottom line here is that there is much, much more to you than has ever been imagined—90% more. Yes, within those blue pills is the spiritual sedative that allows 90% of you to be relegated to the back seat of the car while the old pal ego takes care of your survival instincts.

And there is more that I have left for the next chapter. It's in everyone equally but it ain't working the way it should on Old Earth. Old earth required a lot of dedication and hard work to awaken this. Now, in preparation for New Earth, it is being awakened for all without any effort.

So do you want to serve the gods with only your survival instincts or do you want to be God with these goodies you already have? Your Choice.

9

MORE PARTS OF YOU

The Chakra Antennae

Through time, there is a system of magnetic and unexplainable energy flows within the body that has never ever left the writings of humanity. It is about these things called chakras that are spinning vortexes of energy aligned vertically through and in the physical body. It is hard to find someone these days that does not acknowledge that they exist. And secondly the other change is there are vast amounts of writings that enforce a legitimate tie-in to the physics and chemistry of the physical form. Even medicine is shifting on this topic. Of course science and medicine can't really validate this old knowledge so it rattles around the esoteric world with little support.

But for eons of time, each chakra has been assigned a special purpose and essence in relation to seven major body functions that have a specific vibratory range and also governs certain physical "action" as well as a conscious "essence."

In structure, the vertical line of energy centers goes from a higher vibration of violet, to a lower vibration of red. It also reflects the process of imaginary (above) to physical (below).

CHAKRA	GLAND	COLOR	I	NOTE	ESSENCEe
7 Crown	Pineal	Violet	KNOW	B	Spiritual Connection
6 3rd Eye	Hypo-thalamus	Indigo	SEE	A	Intuition Awareness
5 Throat	Thyroid	Cobalt Blue	SPEAK	G	Commun-ication
4 Heart	Thymus	Green	FEEL	F	Love Expression
3 Solar Plexus	Adrenal	Yellow	WILL	E	Personal Power
2 Sacral	Sexual	Orange	RELATE	D	Sexual Capacity
1 Root	Adrenal	Red	HAVE	C	Survival, Will to Live

It is interesting that over considerable time, the same picture evolves; that these connect between outside influences to inside physical organs effecting behaviour as in the above table. It is like an invisible antennae system that picks up subtle energies and then translates them into some chemical, biochemical or physical result or action.

The seven major chakra centers could be likened to seven electrical batteries or seven dynamic force centers within the physical vessel. You draw forth into these seven power centers the specific qualities, attributes and virtues of the transmitters. The manner in which you qualify and use these energies determines your energetic signature and sets your resonance as to what you are, and how you respond—mentally and physically.

If you look at the progression of these chakras, they go from 3 above the heart to 3 below the heart. And if you look at their overall documented functions, at the top it starts as the mind generates the energy of thoughts, and then projects these outward and inward through the body. The body adds emotion, then creates intent and action, and then connects with the universe to generate an event. A reaction, hence an experience, comes back to you in the form of a perception of that event.

The energy process changes from non-physical to physical as it proceeds from the three above to the three below. These subtle energy centers are known to have a direct affect on seven major groups of physical organs. These organs control the physiological and psychological functions related to the **verb** actions on the left. In other words starting in a non-physical world, you **know** a **thought**, **see** an **image**, **speak** some **words**, and **feel** an **emotion**. This may or may not prompt an action. Assuming an action is prompted, from that point, you move into the physical world. By using intent, you **will** yourself into an **action** which will allow you to **relate** to others and physical **events**, thereby allowing you to **have** a **material** experience. You may be interested to know that I did not invent this. These words and their relation to the chakra energy centers go a long way back into ancient knowledge and are still used today. The process illustrates how subtle energy manifests from a non-physical thought to a material experience. Everybody does this every day. What this also reflects is a time old expression of As above, So below; what is brought into the thoughts is manifested into the reality below.

Notice how the top three chakras are non-physical while the bottom three are physical, with the heart as the balance point. Notice also how the bottom three are essentially ego driven reflecting survival (the will to live, have relations and acquire physical comforts) in the physical world, while the top three are spiritually driven (higher knowledge or Spirit, intuition and truth), reflecting non-physical life concepts.

In the perfect situation, these energy centers are supposed to be balanced by their counterpart. Thus thought (above) balances material (below), image balances events, and words balance actions. They are balanced by the energy system (emotion) of the heart. That is called balancing, alignment, and coherence of subtle energies.

So in the picture of the energy centers, you will note that each **verb** and **subject** can have either a negative or positive attribute. You can **know** a negative or positive **thought** and **have** live a **material** life of **hell** or **heaven.** The idea is that if you want a joyful life, your experiences and perceptions should be focused on the positive energies where harmony, peace, clarity, and joy dominate. That is the perfect world of course. The truth is that these are simply choices you make. You will come to understand that when you choose negative or positive perceptions, trigger thoughts, add emotion, and you send a subtle energy packet out to find more buddies.

By managing these top verbs to produce positive subtle energy packets, you can work towards that perfect world of harmony, a good life and Heaven on Earth. By not managing this process, the energy feedback loop simply responds to whatever thoughts, words and emotions you are sending out by default. The real challenge here is to live a life that always keeps positive stuff in the top three because they create likeness below; and to always react positively from below (experience) as they create more stuff above.

An example of how this works is the sentence *"I love the taste of apple pie."* If we dissect this sentence, the words can be recorded into an electronic signature. Each word also has a signature. The verb love is an emotion and the subject taste from the apple pie is a desire. In subtle energy terms, the thoughts using these words also have a signature.

If an emotion like love is added to the thought, it gets stamped with this quality. If the subject apple pie conjures up magnificent smells and tastes, these can be added to an image of the pie. So if you are sitting day dreaming about apple pie, your emotions get loose and the emotions of love and taste are triggered. Perhaps a nice feeling and your saliva glands get activated. Obviously the word pie creates a physical representation (a material construct) in your mind; the same as the physical pie. A thought is converted into a physical experience in the body.

When these signatures are projected out carrying an emotion or words which have specific physical representations to you, something must be reflected back representing the vibrations of the verbs (emotions) and the subjects (material representation). Depending on how clear the order is that goes out controls how specific the result is that is attracted back.

For example, if you were only projecting the verb (emotion) of fear, then that would attract something that brought more fear. You would have no idea what it would be or when it will occur. We don't remember this or even correlate the event and the emotion. But depending on the strength, somewhere along the line you would encounter another experience of fear.

If there was a specific image along with the emotion, then the reflection process becomes more defined and specific. If the process is all garbled and loose, then obviously nothing can be reflected. In this case you can, by default, be drawn into someone else's experience.

Emotion is of course the most powerful energy and it is universal. That is, a word or an image may bring different interpretations and perceptions in each culture but the emotion of love or compassion attached to the words is not subject to misinterpretation. In a simplistic way, projected energy tries to find a match of something that closely resembles the emotion it was created under. This match brings a physical representation that your brain understands and it brings other subtle energies (like thoughts and ideas) to you.

Interesting it is, that the balance point of this emotion—the most powerful energy—is the heart.

The double Torus

Centered on the heart chakra, and overlaying all chakras is another field known as the double torus of infinity. It is centered on the heart as the engine of energy, the center of singularity. Accept this as a knowing as well. It means your heart is the central engine. Inside this torus is your pillar of life, your chakra system that is not only the transference vehicle between DNA and biology from above to below, but energy transmutation from thought to form both biology and to external material. And so the torus is the spiraling engine that does the actual transmutation of energy. The double torus is like a funnel of energy that spins down the funnel becoming more and more concentrated to reach the singularity point at the heart. Then the funnel inverts itself at the heart and the energy then spins down and expands. This is the double torus.

Each chakra has a function to interface between 3D and other D's within this torus. Your thoughts, images, language, emotions, intent, relationships, existence move down the pillar from above to below and are deployed for the expansion and expression at the choice of consciousness. They are the receivers and transmitters talking to DNA. You have developed a knowing about this. The thoughts, visions, words, emotions that drive intent constitute the torroid process downward to the heart at the point of singularity that then drops into the bottom torroid of intent, relationship and 3D expression of manifestation, and eventually materialization of matter.

The way the pillar is deployed is by choice and intent, and carries the communication of information between consciousness of mind between your first layer of DNA of biological-chemical and the other 11 DNA pairs that constitute your being. This interface is not working at full capacity. It has atrophied through fear and your choice to not develop spiritually into what you are. So it sits stagnant in your DNA. The manifesting processes you have come to know as resident transmitters in your chakras are the thoughts, visions, and the language of emotions. The choice is whether these are sourced from the essence of the heart—love, or the essence of ego—intellect.

Although they are all one, all interconnected, this is a choice of either heart or ego. But nevertheless, all that is you, in your DNA, of karmic lesson, of Divine, of Akashic, and all that is, it all sits awaiting your awareness and intent. You have a knowing that the best interface is positive thought, visions of completion, words of the language of creation, emotion of love and forgiveness. This is speaking, listening, feeling with the heart. For all this means is that the choice of your seeing, speaking, listening, feeling and thinking is always in the light, not with the traditional limited physical sensory system. The portals of access to the DNA is the communication medium of love. And the ability to optimize the torroid's process is the bringing of these positive attributes into the singularity of heart—yes the heart of all matter. This is simply your knowing that it is so, and however this works is not relevant because you acquire the faith and trust that this is so, and all you have to do is accept and be it. The true power of this process is keyed to a specific vibratory range that is what the energy of love is.

So, there is a lot of stuff in you that is your Light Body. Now remember the 100 trillion bits of your DNA that are all in quantum space, all connected, all acting instantly as one? Well, the Light Body is also one of trillions of other bodies that make up the Unity Consciousness. And this Light Body has a certain vibrational signature unique to you.

Us vibrating humans

All things are energies that are vibrating patterns. On the scale, fear is the lowest and unconditional love is the highest. Everything that exists sits in between this and is defined by infinite combinations of patterns. In this sense it is important to understand that all humans have a unique identity signature of human energy that is their aspect of vibration.

Valerie Hunt, a physical therapist and professor of Kinesiology at UCLA, developed a way to confirm and measure the human energy field. For example, Doctors use EEGs and EKGs to measure electrical activities of the brain and the heart. She discovered the EMG or the Electromyograph measures the energy field in muscles and expands into the aura. The normal frequency range in the brain is 0-100cps (cycles per second) most occurring between 0-30cps. Muscle goes to 225cps, heart to 250 but this is where electrical function associated with biology drops off. She picked up a field of energy radiating from the body that ranged between 100 and 1600cps.

These were strongest in the areas of the chakras. She noted the field behaves holographically as do the energy

143

fields of the body and that these fields were non-local—could be measured anywhere on the body. That's the old quantum DNA mist. She called it the holographic field of reality. When the main focus of consciousness is on material, the frequencies are in the lower range around 250cps. People who have psychic abilities and can heal are 400-800cps. People who can go into a trance and channel other information operate in a narrow band of 800-900cps to receive information.

Those who are mystical are above 900cps and these are the ones who possess the wisdom to know what to do with the channeled information as they are aware of cosmic interrelatedness of all things and are in touch with every level of human experience. They are anchored in both psychic and trance abilities, but their frequencies extend beyond up to 200,000cps. You can pretty well figure out where Christ was.

What is quite important here is that this vibrational scale, as exhibited on Old Earth relates to a progression of psychic abilities. If you look at the A-Z of psychic abilities, there are some 200 listed. But the main ones are; after life communications, aparitioning, apportation, astral projection, card reading, channeling, clairvoyant, déjà vu, divining, divine intervention, invisibility, empathy, ESP, levitation, materialization, necromacy, out of body, ouji, past life regression, palmistry, psychic healing, energy healing as in miracles, remote viewing, scrying, tarot, telekinesis, teleportation, telepathy, and transfiguration.

What Valerie is saying and showing is that there is a relationship between the vibrational frequency of the body's electromagnetic system and specific psychic abilities. Yes, these are the esoteric metaphysics type abilities that open. That is what we refer to as *raising one's vibration*! And what is it that raises vibration? Love!

Your crystalline form

Our basic makeup is silica—crystalline based. As a carbon based being, your body is made of in large part carbon. Carbon has some very interesting properties when it is in its physical quantum state. Carbon has 2 orbits of electrons with 4 electrons in the outer shell. Silicon has 3 orbits with 4 in the outer shell. To create silicon from carbon, a new electron must be introduced into the atom and original electrons must be excited into a new orbit. This excitement can be a simple matter. As a carbon based human, each is close to the edge of transformation. Be aware that new electrons can flow into the atoms from the electromagnetic field of the Universe to trigger this transformation.

As the energies coming onto Earth continue to increase vibrations, a critical mass will be reached where electromagnetic frequencies become strong enough to introduce this electron into the atom, thereby exciting the existing ones into the new orbit. Yes, it is that simple. That is an interesting transformation is it not? Your carbon life form receives O_2 and exhales CO_2. Silicon life receives O_2 and exhales (radiates) SiO_2 as pure crystal equivalent to Quartz. Silicon being a semi conductor, and quartz being a natural transmitter, they are capable of receiving and transmitting electromagnetic frequencies. As a silicon body increases vibration, it becomes luminescent, reflecting and refracting light. The Auric field becomes highly charged creating a mini vortex or helix as a spiral of white light. The DNA Merkabah lights on fire!

This proposes the transformation into a new evolutionary form of being that is unique. It would not, however, be some instant transformation. It would be an evolution by choice and most likely occur as the pineal gland, which is itself crystalline in nature, evolves. In this scenario a time will come when new ascended consciousness simply activates the intention to bring in these extra electrons and transform into play as many are transforming now. But this new being of light would have no need to reproduce. It would live forever, communicate telepathically, have all the abilities of an ascended one like Christ and be able to transform into any physical 3D energy form at will.

This is a being that will evolve with expanded abilities beyond the list of metaphysical, those that have not been comprehended yet. These will be activated and imbedded into physicality as part of the DNA signatures of all beings; but not many will take to the calling. This is beginning to show in the physical plane as the Crystal Children who are in structure expanded and semi-crystalline beings in transition. Their abilities go beyond what the usual Lower Selves can comprehend and they are born this way fully open because they are coming in at a higher vibration—one that Old Earther's don't understand. Most of humanity and the Lower Selves are not able to deal with this and therefore it is discouraged and subdued for reasons of fear and being non-traditional scary stuff. The kids don't fit the old mould, but ironically it is the kids that are creating the new mould. But many adults at an advanced stage of ascension are rising to this to open a path for these millions of beings that are filling the planet. It is part of the greater plan.

It will be a slow evolution for most as the lower human form of carbon merges with the silicon that is higher based vibration. As the abilities and needs change, the old habits of the lower form begin to drop away as ego does not survive. It is not needed here and the old ways of struggle vanish and drop away as not necessary. And what is needed is created or experienced at will in an upper domain of love and light. The senses and abilities not only expand on the physical body which can in the beginning function somewhat as now, but a choice comes forward of simply dropping the traits of the old ways like eating, reproduction, struggling, conflict and taking on new ways to replace these. In affect this becomes a hybrid cross between the true self of Light Being and an "atomic" body for physical expression.

Fear cannot exist here, nor does polarity in this being which because of its higher makeup and awareness is a multidimensional, transcended, transmuting creator of matter, which is only holographic. The awareness of the hologram and how it works in the cosmic laws will reveal itself as vibration rises and the knowing of Self eliminates lower vibrations like fear. The higher vibratory plane and its interdimensional abilities make it resilient to the darker energies that attempt to invade or change it. The brightness that shines from this being as the higher love and light simply lights darkness to show to all what energies true purpose is—instantly. As you know, when light or truth shines on darkness or deception, the dark energies fade in power and intent or take on the illumination.

There are those who will lead this to bring awareness to others in ways to show the Lower Selves the way by example—in the love and light of service and the new ascension. Are you prepared for this?

The silent assimilation

The new chakra system has already begun its assimilation into Higher and Lower bodies. This is a 5th dimensional system already pre-loaded with triggers to talk to DNA and trigger interdimensional higher abilities. It will be triggered to entrain Higher and Lower bodies into one drawing them together into higher vibrational planes as they begin to sing together. The time is right now and it is best to simply let this be by intent and evolve with it.

As this opens and each chakra draws information that it already has access to in the DNA, each will draw what is pertinent to it alone, entraining this to the normal chakra system and providing the necessary signals to translate into the physical and chemical processes needed for transformation of cellular structure. This will then be up to the Higher Mind to activate when it feels proper. Each will open and in so doing awaken DNA to reshape, and revitalize your cellular structure.

Your DNA is already encoded with special characteristics from highly evolved DNA from other crystalline beings of light in the galaxy but not ready for awakening. The new singing of the crystalline structure to the new chakras will begin to resonate and DNA will respond to give it life. This has been triggered, and by intent it will so complete into a wondrous evolution of Self.

What will develop is awareness of the 5D parallel world that has formed where we are all one with the Source. This will first open to you during your sleep time as your intent and attention to it will respond this time with full awareness and memory of it. You will receive information into your chakras, be with us to learn with other beings and learn about your hologram, and allow

148

your lower self to properly adjust to this new world and develop your ability to straddle both. It is unlike anything you can comprehend so your Higher Mind will decide how.

Now the big question? How much control do you think you have on an ascension process and how it unfolds? Do you control the stock market consciousness or do you react and follow it?

Remember that conscious intent is the most powerful of all and the heart field is the one that can change quantum to non quantum. The only control you have is to pretend you have not heard any of this and refuse the Train Ticket. But sorry, it will not stop what's happening.

The big question is whether you want to be on board or not? Do you want to try to avoid this and serve gods or do you want to be God? Your Choice.

10

THE UPPER AND LOWER PATHS

The Hopi Prophesy of End Times

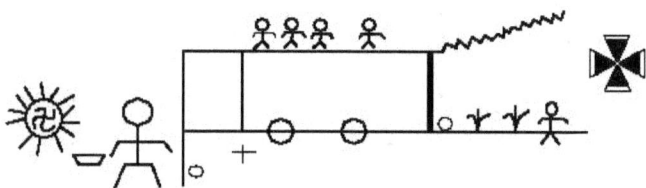

Near Oraibi, Arizona, there is a petroglyph known as Prophecy Rock which symbolizes many Hopi prophecies. Its interpretation is:

The large human figure on the left is the Great Spirit. The bow in his left hand represents his instructions to the Hopi to lay down their weapons. The vertical line to the right of the Great Spirit is a time scale in thousands of years. The point at which the Great Spirit touches the line is the time of his return. The "life path" established by the Great Spirit divides into the lower, narrow path of continuous Life in harmony with nature and the wide upper road of white man's scientific achievements. The bar between the paths, above the cross, is the coming of white men; the Cross is that of Christianity. The circle below the cross represents the continuous Path of Life. The four small human figures on the upper road represent, on one level, the past three worlds and the present; on another level, the figures indicate that some of the Hopi will travel the white man's path, having been seduced by its glamour. The two circles on the lower Path of Life are the "great shaking of the earth" (interpreted to be World Wars One and Two by the wise Hopis). The swastika in the Sun and the Celtic cross represent the two helpers of Pahana, the True White Brother.

The short line that returns to the straight Path of Life is the last chance for people to turn back to nature before the upper road disintegrates and dissipates. The small circle above the Path of Life, after the last chance, is the Great Purification, after which corn will grow in abundance again when the Great Spirit returns and the Path of Life continues forever. The Hopi shield in the lower right corner symbolizes the Earth and the Four-Corners area where the Hopi have been reserved. The arms of the cross also represent the four directions in which they migrated according to the instructions of the Great Spirit. The dots represent the four colors of Hopi corn, and the four racial colors of humanity. After the Great Purification, one path disintegrates into chaos, the other continues forever.

Admittedly there are many interpretations of this but they consistently reflect a need for choice at some point. There are three ways to go here and it relates to the New Earth scenario that is upon us. You can stay in Old Earth and the Lower Path to serve the gods or you can take the Higher Path and New Earth to Ascension and be God. Or perhaps you may want to overcome both of these and try the path that has been prevalent for some time on planet Earth—that of Dominion, trying to be one of those gods that the helpless serve.

Ascension is the Higher Path

The Higher Path is the one the Ascension Train Ticket to New Earth takes you to. It is the progression of higher vibration from the awakening to the ascension. The gifts are along the train ride as of the awakenings in your Lower Self, DNA and in your body, mind, and chakra energy systems. As the Higher Divine Mind takes its command it knows how to progress and at what pace to expand just as your Lower Mind knows what pace or limits to impose to guide you in a physical or learning activity in your regular 3D life. This higher path of learning and physical adjustment is no different except that the Higher Mind guides with the heart from a higher perception through divine inspiration and practice, always being within the higher vibration of the One.

The signs along the path come to you as your higher body chakra system cast away imbalance and dysfunction by your attention and will to open to their true functions of expanded senses and abilities. Let us start from the main chakras from the bottom.

Your lower one is the Earth chakra. It is below you encapsulating you, and connecting your ether double to the Mother Gaia. It is your grounding, drawing the nourishment of the Mother to you. As it awakens, it firmly connects your being between it and the upper most chakra above you which is the connection to the One, the Source; Heaven. It is the heart that balances these two. As the awareness of these three opens, the flow between them allows the others to awaken to their full potential. The awakening and balancing of these chakras is what is happening now.

To see the shift from above (thinking) to below (physical) it can be described this way. At the Root, the awakening brings the knowing that you are part of all that is Gaia and all living things. It is about it all being One. The sense of completion, of wholeness opens here as a reality. At the Sacral level, the wholeness is expanded by the reverence and the wonder of you and the relationship to the whole—to Gaia and what she and all living things are and being all interconnected. The importance of the wondrous relationship expands here. At the Solar Plexus level, this connection to all is of the knowing of the will and the action and intent by way of the power of the intuition; that how you relate is sensed here as to what is right in the relationship and aligned with the heart.

At the Heart level, the emotion, the feelings of love and compassion prevail as being drawn by the nature of a true empathic relationship to all that is you and the One. It is your feeling and healing center, one of knowing and sensing the discord so that it can be cleansed, healed or brought back to a state of perfection—in perfect alignment with the heart and the Source.

At the Throat level, it is all about communications with all that is, it is the ability to telepathically connect with all living things and to sense their states of evolution and purpose. At the 3rd Eye it is about seeing all that is and all within it by the attention to it. At the Crown it is about the connection to all that is to the knowing of all that was, is and will be. It is the connection to the God Source of all knowledge and knowing. At the very top is your Heaven chakra, the portal to the Universe to interdimensionality and the connection to the Father, the source of the spark of life itself. The process is one of replacing the physical sensory system with the etheric double or chakra sensory system, or what is known as shifting to the Heart.

These all expand as your Upper Path evolves and the body begins to change, dropping many of your material and physical needs. As the high side of each chakra wakens, the lower side drops away or fades in importance and as your abilities open to those you are practicing now, you begin to co-create in your lower world and you begin to shift your attention to the higher world—as you are finding now in your Interdimensional sessions. These as you see now have no bounds. They are but a tiny part of what is unfolding. As you progress on this path, you learn to walk both worlds. What you originally believed to be imagination and a fabrication, is not. Your physical body becomes lighter and of the Light and it is able to drop its many needs like food and air and other things that your etheric double—your Higher Body—does not require. And it will take you into these upper cosmic planes that you begin to experiment with as you do now. You will be able to bring this body with you at will thereby bringing Earth to Heaven.

At the same time, you as your Higher Mind and Body will bring what you learn and know of Heaven in the upper dimensions to Earth. Yes, all balanced and commanded by the heart—the command center between Heaven and Earth—the Father and Mother. These worlds become interchangeable at will. Along the path are your road signs and markers. You are seeing these markers as your own telepathy, healing, channelling, galactic travel and manifestation skills forming the as above so below interaction. These are unfolding on you and thus enfold a new life upon you. You are at that stage of the expanded phase of the journey, where the partnership with the

Divine and entry to the other side on the High Path is your reality. After the intent of the Train Ticket, particularly during the entry to New Earth and Resurrection, this path unfolds rapidly with the assistance of many cosmic forces.

Descension is the Lower Path

The lower path is a choice of any who will ignore the calling of ascension. All you do here is to reject the intent of taking the ticket and keep gobbling the blue pills. The process which unfolds will be the same as others on the upper path up to a point. Up to this point some new surprising abilities will open. These, which have been thought of as metaphysical or esoteric nonsense will develop in all at the cellular DNA level. They may be used, feared, ignored, and many may attempt to commercialize or use these for their own dominion or fame. But many will not.

And when the healing, telepathy, empathy and manifestation begin to rise in all, any advantages or dominion will cease, as will the drive to commercialize for profit. Motivations will be easier read as the intuition and energy reading improve. As the ascension quickens on these, resistance or fear may manifest itself faster as will all thoughts and feelings but others like you will be there to explain this and to assist in the graceful shift of mind to the way of the heart.

Some may not heed or want to change their ways and they will continue on the old awakening path bringing upon them lessons of dis-ease and discord faster and faster until they recognize the reasons of cosmic laws. It is no different than now and their lives will take a normal traditional path of reincarnation. They will simply be reborn again in a different hologram. The ones who remain on this path will be crowded out and the consciousness of the new will begin to resonate stronger and stronger as the evolution continues and the eventual melding occurs. On the upper path, the evolution accelerates creating more and more that will teach and more and more that will raise the mass consciousness vibration faster. Also relevant here on the lower path is the Law of Infliction that has been covered before.

At any part of the lower path, a choice is always there to partner with the Divine heart and move to the Light side as the contrast between the paths will become more obvious and visible, impossible for the establishment to ignore and the process will begin to switch as a minority will usually follow the majority. The major change will be that the majority will teach spiritual sovereignty where no one has dominion in the laws of the One and Infliction. At first, those who stay on the lower path— those that have not reached the vibratory level of the Divine Self and Heart, will leave their bodies as is now.

They may be recycled back but only as the new crystalline essence as are newborns now. There will be a point where only the recycling occurs and no new souls are needed on the Old Earth but in any case, the DNA will be fully activated in these, coming into an evolving consciousness of new mass consciousness, knowing the truth and being supported in the new energies, already wired for ascension. This process will begin to shift Gaia and her relationship with humanity. How this unfolds is not written, and what Gaia chooses to leave along this holographic path is up to her and the symbiant consciousness of the living things upon her.

There is, however, a minority of power lords who are of the dark and dominion over others. We will speak of this next.

Dominion is the self destruct path

There is an option along the lower path. It is for those that choose dominion and control over others. This may be because you choose this path because you believe that this ascension stuff is nonsense and it provides a great opportunity to improve your 3D position of ego, wealth, and power over others that you may deem as foolish sheep. It may be because your DNA is so encoded with the lower vibration it continues to be void of spirit, it cannot be awakened, or that you believe the heart alignment and Divine is a weakness.

It can be triggered easily in you and the ones responsible for activating this within you are well advanced in the cosmic ways of energy being able to manipulate humanity this way. They are of course void of spirit by choice as they know that by creating fear of death, pain, loss or discomfort or insecurity, it invokes low vibrational energies of cosmic law to bring more upon you to prevent ascension and awareness that you are more than this low vibration. Knowing also that part of humanity's DNA encoding is to seek a greater power, by manipulating the religions, they attempt to satisfy this draw but also control it to deceive. Yes, that is the way of it.

They are ones who are of the knowing of the working of vibrational energies and the different dimensions. They, who know how to use this to keep humanity in the lower state are in for a big surprise. Through time they have been successful in this by taking dominion and control through this process of subduing spiritual, physical, and commercial sovereignty—but not so through the Law of Infliction.

If we speak of these dimensions, they understand how to work in the higher invisible etheric planes of energy within the holograms. For a simple example, many are learning that they are within a physical material plane of 3D. They are learning that energies of potential congealment are in a temporary transitional state of 4D. The 5D plane is where the Higher Self also is as it reaches across all dimensions but like the physical body, may not yet be awake. As these people can now understand, the thoughts and energies they create begin in 5D with attention, action and intent, waiting in 4D, ready to manifest in 3D. As above, so below. This is a simple example of course but this is the way creators as the God Self create in the hologram—the level of creation being your level of vibration. The ones who prefer dominion and are heartless know and have used this well in humanity's lessons.

Of course, those who choose to control, know they can control without conscience of the heart or spirit by avoiding the heart with exception of their own blood lines. This will be their undoing. Thus they can kill, threaten, raise fear and bring conflict without mercy or compassion as dominion becomes their passion. They have also learned that subliminal devices, and many ways of triggering the dark energies can be used to confuse, change and reshape the transitional energies of 4D and also confuse the purpose of the Higher Self of body and mind at the 5D level. However so will everybody else! So the gig is up!

New Earth is where the Divine Higher Self exists and it is immune to such things because of its higher vibrational plane that cannot support lower energies. And then, on top of this, the ones who know the gig is up may also come to Old Earth to spill the beans; if the Law of Infliction has not yet taken its toll.

So what is your choice? Upper, Lower or Dominion? Serve gods, pretend to be a god or be God? Your Choice.

11

LOVE, LAUGH, LIVE AS ONE HEART

The true secret is Love

What is important to really understand is that the traditional path to enlightenment—the one that Christ and many others achieved—has been difficult on Old Earth. It is not so this time during the End Times. Over the ages, many, many, esoteric practices, cults, traditions, and wisdoms, have evolved as humanity seeks enlightenment. Back in the Mystery Schools of Egypt, even Christ had to wrestle with this growth of karma and lesson, of overcoming the draw of the flesh, of ego. That is the way it was.

In the current day because there is a tsunami of this unity consciousness flooding humanity, there are zillions of products around, with millions of experts that have gizmos and secret ways to heal your dysfunctional body, help you extend life, find unbelievable wealth and happiness. Is this in itself not a wakeup call to a new consciousness?

None of this is needed.

The more you seek this, the more you engage in seeking. Remember, that is the way of energy manifestation. Seeking a solution is work, negative energy that in itself keeps you seeking. The solution is already in you so stop seeking. And at this special time, no one has to sit like a monk in celibacy on a mountain top most of his life trying to be enlightened to seek the solution. Unless, of course, you ignore this gifting that is upon you.

All you have to do is create the intent of allowing the process to unfold and to enjoy the train ride.

This is the ultimate secret of life revealed during the Time of Choosing. All you have to do is understand and accept that which some simple words like being in the heart and unconditional love mean. That is not so simple if you cannot believe a new way is upon you. Nor is living your mortal life the way of the heart a simple matter if you are entrenched in ego's attachments.

Your true being sits in a place that is your heaven. You sit there as an aspect of the Creator as a piece of its total consciousness which is a quantum substance of love. As an analogy, it is like your currently local 3D mind that has no clear definition or substance. It simply exists and you know this because it drives your process of thinking and acting.

Here you sit as this Higher Mind as a Being of Light watching a lower aspect of you in Old Earth playing out a movie drama of life. You watch and you wonder; when will he or she know the secret of what is already known? You watch this mortal in its lower form evolving slowly but struggling with physicality, strength, body, age, health which takes much attention. You watch the dealings with issues of money, of family, of things that are seemingly so unfair with the suffering of others, the unjust dominion of the elite beings, and the long story of the slavery of humans. And you wonder why he or she has not implemented the secret yet.

And you think and project upon this lower form of physicality some information in the hope it can listen. It is this information of question and answer; What is it that cannot be solved by love? How can you change your life? Love. How do you heal your body? Love. How do you find bliss? Love. How can you heal the planet? Love. How can you materialize physicality? Love. How do you ascend? Love. How do you open to your fullest Creator abilities? Love. Is there anything that cannot be solved by love? And what is it that is infinitely abundant that is the true power of the universe? Love.

The secret is unconditional love. It is the highest vibration of all things. It is the vibration of the Creator and the makeup of all Creation, that is what you struggle to rise to. As Creator, your vibration is pure, absolute and the highest possible. That is the end of it. What you do in 5D in the essence of love is the same in 3D. The lessons are to teach you to rise above, to attain the degree of power through the level of vibration. Do you know that as a Creator, you can overlay a thought grid upon Gaia that will affect the physical behavior of all humanity?

This is a large responsibility is it not? It is not done by those that are not of the highest, purest vibration of heart, and without the knowing of your soul group and Divine mind. That is all there is to this. In 3D absolutely every moment must be pure unconditional Divine love; that's it, nothing else. Ask yourself what cannot be solved by love. So what is it that slows you? Immerse into the purity of love—nothing else—Oneness of All That Is. The alignment of you with the God Consciousness is the first step, and to know who you are.

The next step is the degree of purity which is the level of vibration. It is reflected in everything you do in your physical form. Once it is aligned as one aspect, and the strength of that absoluteness is your very being, all your issues are solved—permanently. No secrets, nothing but love.

A new Job?

It is what Christ rose to. It is what the Christ Consciousness gifts you. And this time there is no struggle, no convincing others, no opposition because it's *all happening to all at the same time*.

There is a new job for you. First get your Train Ticket. It is your conscious intent to live in a New Earth of unconditional love and be God. Throw the blue pills away and burn the prescription.

Then place your Trust and Faith not in others but in yourself. Don't look for instant miracles for it is a transition. During this transition here is your new "job".

You have a charged Heart Light and it is to shine light upon any darkness that you may come upon. It draws your love and shines where your new Darkness Detection Device in your heart senses darkness. It is best that as you do your daily surveillance of darkness that you use your new hovercraft of your etheric body which allows being above so you are not engaged directly. Here you can have a direct top view of any darkness.

What you receive in return for shining your Heart Light is joy. Your heart is connected to Source heart so you have an infinite supply of light and love to shine, and the process of converting to joy is like a current flow. It is what allows your craft to stay in its higher plane and the conversion process of changing darkness (negative) to joy (positive) is a flow of current that affects the brightness of your heart AND your DNA bulb which contains your total signature and it awakens. And the stronger the flow of conversion to bliss, the brighter is your bulb and the lighter is your body.

Sometimes you may feel it is appropriate to land and engage with others to feel joy and also become brighter on the ground. But remember that by engaging in lower experiences with others sometimes the light may cast shadows where darkness hides itself. Of course these are moments that are opportunities to reap the joy but you must be mindful not to attach or allow attachment. The brightness of your bulb here is very powerful as it can be felt by others around you. Each moment is there for you to enjoy the encounter and provide a possible moment to convert into the current to enhance your brightness. You know how to deploy your new senses in all your 3D affairs for this to expand your DNA to its full brightness and it will then entrain the body within it from its lower form upwards into higher form.

That is all you have to do in your new job.

The power is in the Heart

Over the ages, the heart has received a lot of press. Heartless, heart of a lion, heartfelt, with all my heart, the list is endless. What's the infatuation with this thing that's a physical pump?

It ain't just a pump; it, like everything else of your being has an invisible, quantum counterpart of energy. You can go back and review the chapter of what you are but the heart is the link between who you are as an immortal Being of Light and who you are as a mortal being of holographic substance—material form. That's what it is all about.

And if you don't think there is power there, just think about the process of being in love, or protecting your children. Think about the physical and mental power that these reflect. Heartfelt, love from the bottom of my heart, heart of a lion? It's not that pump that instigates the behavior is it?

The simplicity of all is that essence of above of God, love, heart all reside in the heart center as the expression vehicle of lower form. It is to practice this learning turned to knowing that becomes your path to mastery. Yes, *love, laugh, and live as One Heart*. The heart is the key to all that is, mastering the space between and of all that is; knowing and showing of what you are, a heart of expression. Every moment that comes before the heart is one to cast light of love upon, get a joyous laugh, and in so doing create the flow of pure life in its Divine essence. This means to be in it, to connect it, to live it, and to maintain it in a state of joy and bliss. This is what your prime purpose is, and so you allow as one with all to expand and experience the prime essence of Divine love.

So you say it doesn't pay the bills? Well, first change the rules of engagement in your working efforts. Don't *expect* an instant transfer from God's bank to yours. Then begin your new job with your heart light, knowing a transfer will occur—then watch what happens.

There is no greater power as it is the supreme power and it cannot be subjected to, or be below dominion, nor can it be used for that purpose. It is the link and the conduit between God and you as part of God. As you live every moment in the heart, to love, to laugh, the return is bliss and joy. The heart is the conduit between the 3D world of body and the higher divine mind which is God. It cannot be fooled and it is all knowing, simply being patient for you to know and to show how to love, laugh, live every moment within it. Yes it is so.

The pull to perfection

Through the Time of Choosing pay attention to a shift. You will feel a pull of perfection and the New Earth upon you as an overlay on the Old Earth, forming itself as the new hologram. It is subtle and you feel it as you walk with it in your consciousness, when you see, hear, speak, feel that around you. You are beginning to drop your attention to the discord and darkness as it does not vibrate within you now, except to point out what is not right of heart, and you may feel the empathy, of sorrow yet it does not engage you to bring forward fear, lack, anger or lower emotions and vibrations for these are losing their hold on you to engage.

You are losing the attention to old energies as being important and you look to the beauty, the reverence, the joy of senses, and laughter as your moments pass before you. You look to alternatives that give you peace and intuitive comfort. You sense your body's shifting as it does not work the same and is sensitive in new places as it is shifting; yet you know not what is happening. The affairs of masculine and feminine extreme energies seem diminished—like a balancing—yet you cannot explain these moods that are softer.

And you are looking inward, into yourself for answers, for things of joy that are suddenly noticeable that have no price tag and are not in the stores, free of will to experience at the flick of the mind. All things of matter are beginning to look different. Yes it is the new hologram energizing itself from 4D and it is your new form shifting and adjusting. Yet it is subtle—God's plan is subtle as it sneaks upon you and yet you know. There is no time here, no scheme, no deception, only the granting of divine gifts for all.

Think of this as you ask how this can all occur in such a short time, as you look down upon the discord. It has been transitioning for a long time, you have not seen it. It has been the *Matrix*. Now you begin to sense you are the One and you pay attention to your heart, your life, your powers to perceive, to express, to manifest, to create. Allow yourself to shift first as you will then assist others in your revelations.

Find new ways to live your life. Sit down and go through your day's moments and let your heart see, feel, speak, think, hear, sense and act. Do this from your chair as you imagine your perfect day, then go out into your old world and do this as you walk the moments of your day. This is what is happening to all of humanity now—it has begun, the revelations as a subtle energy poured upon consciousness.

All humanity has entered a time of special allowing like none ever before. No karma, no need for lesson, no need for devices, for contraptions to ascend or open DNA, only pure intent and love. Just say so and believe it. And there is no need to heed those who proclaim special wisdom and affiliation with gods, those who pretend to know God's will, for it is all within, waiting to pour out. There is no need for pain or suffering to receive lesson. All is opened for all of humanity equally and all of the cosmic and divine energy is poured upon all in the grandest time of revelation of all time. All that is needed is your free will to choose to accept and be what you are—love. That is you pulling now, you feel it but cannot explain it. And it is only the beginning.

Think, see, hear, feel, act with the heart

We have all been seeing, hearing, thinking, feeling and launching intention to acting with our mortal beings. It is ego, it is survival, it is using the physical sensors of body. But as you now hopefully understand there is a counterpart of immortal form overlaying this body form—exactly like there is a New Earth overlaying the old. The Old Earth lower mind is being replaced by the New Earth higher mind and instead of the brain being the physical control center it is the heart that becomes the physical command center.

The new configuration of heart and higher mind shifts command to what is New Earth and the old senses of hear, see, feel, etc. give way to a huge range as picked up by the partners of the chakra system that links to the transformed physical (higher vibration). That process that knows only love and unity is to open to the heart. It is to align into the higher carrier wave of all that is, made of the substance of love.

What this means in practice is to take every moment that comes before you and to deploy these new senses to act like a filter of energies of thoughts, visions, words and feelings coming in and to act as the generator of its higher vibration going out of you. This is the energy that you accept or create within your hologram. The filter is to convert all coming in to something positive or good by seeing, hearing, saying, feeling the good part only. That is through the heart. The generator is to create energies going out from the heart that are good, based in love, unconditional—as you would with your own children. The difference here is that everything that is, is your own children. So all you have to do is join hearts, like you do with your family. But your family has grown to New Earth.

No one needs to buy devices, gizmos, or stuff that promises you a DNA awakening, new health and wealth. This is a realm that is accessible through the heart. It is free like the Train Ticket to Ascension. It is all being given to you if you wake up and accept it. You don't even have to work for it, but you have to work at it.

It's unstoppable, it is only a question of choice—yours. Will you now like to stay behind and serve the gods or would you be God? Your Choice!

12

GOD WILL LOVE YOU DESPITE YOURSELF

Know this:

Whatever you choose, there is no judgment attached to your choice. Nor is there a judgment day.

In fact, all of this shifting between Old and New Earths will be subtle at first. It will begin like a new global marketing strategy where the mass consumer simply shifts his attention. But as the new energy floods in, so it replaces the old and many large systems lose their ability to be sustained. It is like the financial and religious systems that are based on debt and dominion— an energy that can't stay anchored in this shifting consciousness.

In addition, a lot of big environmental things like the Japan situation will continue to happen as the shift occurs to highlight old errors of our old system and these become catalysts to change fast as people perish in the lesson. These are areas of old energy dysfunction and deception that get cleared in mass. The shifting from old to new will be like this up until the Time of Transformation when many physical changes to humans and Earth begin their new emergence. It is when the cosmic forces begin to make the old forms strain in an effort to adapt to a changing atmospheric and consciousness environment.

What to expect

There is a very deep resistance within humanity to believe in cosmic influences, despite the fact that the majority of humanity support the stories of Genesis and Christ; these could easily equal the best science fiction story of all time. The ascension process is a global and cosmic phenomenon which quickens now. It is through the influence of the harmonics of cosmic bodies such as the Sun and the Moon as well as other cosmic bodies and energies that are in configurations and energy influencing patterns like in no other time. The ancient science of astrology has atrophied in its attention similar to humanity's own sensory abilities.

Like electrons, celestial bodies orbit along their paths with an essence and energy of their being and in so doing resonate or ring their unique vibrations that emanate from them. For example, all are used to understanding the moon and its gravitational and emotional pull or influence. It is both a physical and mental influence on energies of matter and non-matter, or consciousness. It is because you are 90% energetic in nature.

And so these cosmic bodies are like balls swung on a string near your ears. The vibration of it becomes louder and stronger as it approaches, entraining with specific parts of you that are receptive to it—like your chakras in particular. All cosmic bodies and things create different resonances of vibration and have different unique purposes that are projected, affecting Gaia and all living things to some degree. This becomes more or less intense depending upon its distance, alignment with others, and position away, all to induce a specific pattern. Their individual and joint vibrations that they emanate can affect your consciousness which is itself energy in a wave form transmitted through the chakras to the physical body, affecting biochemistry and behaviour. It is all about interacting energies that we have no control over.

There are many, many such cycles and influences of this nature that come and go to combine into different patterns setting an underlying consciousness environment for all living things. And some of these are very long indeed. We also emit energy patterns with characteristics of vibration with our own heart field— our unique signatures. The effect of course is different on each that receives it or comes under the influence. Many forms exist such as with heat, ultraviolet, infrared, and special cosmic particles of energy are felt by you and their characteristics are known by science. But the characteristics of love, or compassion or spirit are not so obvious to you. They are nevertheless the same, emanating as wave vibrations upon the bodies and minds of all living energies, in different ways or intensity depending upon the vibrational or resonant makeup of each. At the root of this is the strongest force that manages how it is received and transmitted—intent.

It is important to understand there are influences and energies at play here that are all interacting to contribute to the overall influence of consciousness on the planet, irrespective of whether these are 3D, 4D, or 5D states. Such cycles and alignments affect your seasons, your growth and expansion of all living things.

This knowledge of the star systems and the cosmic influences were handed down from ancient knowledge to many who have retained it in some form. The Mayans are the more known but this is also written and known on other continents with the Tibetans, Egyptians, American Indians, and many others. The Mayans were very knowledgeable and understood the workings as related to their growing seasons and life within it. They were conscious of the influences and knew of the longer cycles and alignments of cosmic forces. Thus they indeed knew of the point of 2012 as the time when the shift to a new age would occur from material time to no time—a time when the overall resonance would reach a zenith and a shift into a new consciousness would complete.

This has to do with the ascension of Gaia and those symbiant to her. It involves the influence of vibrations that flood her and you from cosmic neighbours; and from her own larger living body of which she is but a part. These cosmic influences and cycles are vibrations that are influencing the ascension and these are of a nature that you have not yet understood, such as the energy of love and of unity, of spirit and wholeness, of the Light of the Creator—the One. It is of the rising of love and the higher energies that set the scene and the background to Gaia's movie being played out. And as you are symbiant to her, as One, are influenced to some degree.

As Gaia moves into her galactic alignment which is a cycle of 26000 years, it is part of a large portion of an intergalactic cycle of 12 times that. And as Earth approaches the zenith, the influence and hence the pace of potential change quickens as the resonance strengthens. The influence of the bodies, their characteristics and their unique emanations increase as the alignment approaches the maximum. Then a new setting begins to take over and the old world fades. This is all part of the energies delivered to Earth as the new age of influence of Aquarius. This is not an instant process. It is strengthening of new and weakening of old vibrational influence, like the pull of the moon on your oceans—and your consciousness.

As individual units of consciousness and energetic bodies, each human has their own vibrational signatures that entrain with the larger settings and bodies in different degrees and different specific effects—but yet all the same in a larger overall scope.

This is now at a point where the influences and alignments quicken as the zenith of many influences combine in unique configurations that project specific essences of behaviour and physical transformation. If you do not believe this, think about x-rays, ultraviolet, infrared rays. There are many others that affect consciousness. They will begin to override the ego's dominion of these forces. It is the 2012 time where the zenith is reached and it is the point where the greatest influence upon Gaia and her living things is created.

It is important to understand that this process is already well underway. And all are affected to some degree but because each has free will as creator Beings of Light, each can choose how they align with this. They can choose their path and the degree to which they accept the influences of consciousness. Not all will ascend with Gaia and they will live out their lives according to the energies they create. She, like many other creatures, does not have the option. Even though the influences and the body changes to your consciousness come to your awareness, this does not mean that you have to choose the higher path.

The process can be one of a graceful transition and evolution into a new spiritual age of enlightenment and expansion. Or it can be filled with fear and destruction. But whether it is a direct revelation or through others, each comes to a knowing of their place as the equal of Christ. In this respect they can accept that they are an eternal being, that their chosen hologram is one of perfection, and that the parallel world of New Earth is indeed real, awaiting a choice of how and when each enters it. It will become increasingly real on the upper path, especially for those who learn to walk both. However, they can reject this as well. There is no judgement except from one's self.

It is Gaia's time to ascend and move into her rightful place as it is yours if you so choose. It is a process that is set in the Mind of God and its cosmic workings. As it is all One, you are part of the ascension process as is all else. But the choices each individual conscious being makes, and the path chosen, and the way it is to unfold into the life that is completed upon Gaia's, is not decided. It is each that must choose.

The final message

Can you afford to ignore the Train Ticket? There are indeed the Upper and Lower Paths of the ascension choices that unfold before all. Both paths receive the same amount of Light of the One and the ascension energy of awakening. It is all equal but the attention and the awareness to it is very different. As Gaia ascends her own physical body changes as her Higher Essence draws the lower form upwards into the light. This will mean, like your own body, that the body will lighten and begin to change its properties as well.

This proceeds towards the Grand Alignment of 2012 within the Galactic system to align Gaia's heart with others and the Galactic center of heart known as the center of the Milky Way. As the characteristics change and reach the zenith those energies that are not aligned with this fade and dissolve away, transmuted into the dominant energy of the Light and Love of the Source. Those energies that are not compatible will change and shift upon Gaia and the consciousness of humanity that enfolds her. Just as lower forms of energy do not exist in the higher realms, so it is with the negative and darker energies of control, dominion and conflict.

The essence moves to the central heart of the Galaxy and aligns. These lower energies lose their strength as attention to the new shifts and the awareness and attention increases. At the same time, Gaia's properties shift in terms of her physical nature, affecting weather, temperature, water, air, and she begins to glow and shine within her larger body and her scope within the universe expands. Many old energies and devices and material things will begin to be dysfunctional and irrelevant, not supported by the new ways. These will be replaced by the new, more in alignment with the consciousness of the One and all being in harmony with her. These new ways and energies are already surrounding Gaia.

As the consciousness opens and cosmic neighbours open the new awareness, new discoveries, processes compatible with Gaia's changing body will be embraced and brought forward. Many are ready to meet this calling and many are ready to lead and show the new way. The Crystal Children will awaken and emerge to take their rightful place as they will feel the draw with a deepness and strength that will bewilder those that are not awakened. They will teach their knowing and their advanced abilities as the ones of the Higher Path are learning and doing. As this process evolves and quickens towards the alignment of galactic hearts with the heart of One, many changes will occur. The old energy of polarity will fade and a new leader will emerge under the command of their Higher Divine Selves.

Now you walk in the 3D world and are learning to walk differently in your Higher World. This is not yet congealed but has formed through the joint consciousness of those who are awakened and increasing in numbers rapidly, having chosen the Upper Path. What many others are doing now is learning to walk both paths. Look for these as they will come forward as did Christ. This world that is forming has no limits and it is the learning of bringing the heavier body to the higher realm that is coming to attention. As below, the way of it is to have the Higher Mind and Body brought consciously to live upon Gaia and bring limitless possibilities to her and the totality of all humanity as family which is all that is One. Over time a convergence of this will occur. This is the ascension that is an unstoppable process.

Through this immediate period there will be those that sleep or resist, who will not awaken, as there are those that will work to impede the ascension as it does not serve their cause. This simply will not continue. They have become subservient to their needs of power and their DNA is dormant. The conflict of this dark and light will become resolved as more and more light shines upon you, Gaia, and them. As these energy forces clash, as they are now, over the next years the strain of polarity will be felt, both on Gaia and her living things and this will also reach its zenith. The process is one of underlying fading dark energy strength while the light energy is strengthening. During this period it is important to understand that the dark ones are attempting to take desperate means to counteract and to confuse this new consciousness, using devices, technology and their knowledge of the higher worlds so as to flood dysfunction and generate lower energies as Gaia shifts. It is simply the lessons to be learned.

Through the confusion of energy change, all you need to understand is that as the new consciousness grows and floods Gaia, the old fades, one replacing the other. Together these energies of conscious purpose and type create the whole of the influences of consciousness. As one fades, the new replaces and as the new increases to the zenith at the Grand Galactic Heart alignment, eventually all of the old will be replaced. As this proceeds, the crystalline structure will slowly move each away from the usual 3D body requirements, especially any that are not aligned with the Higher Divine mind and heart. This is the Higher Path that can be chosen **but you need to choose.**

But, and here is the big but.

Right now, as has always been, there is an invisible world that each of us as a mere mortal human cannot see, nor understand. We have simply denied its existence by indulging in the mortal life. It is the quantum world that has always been there and will always be. The entry to it has always been the same—by a conscious awareness of its existence and by a knowing, and acceptance of who you are. The process of change, from Old Earth which is visible, to New Earth which is not, is essentially a transparent process up to a point. Up to a point of merging all will appear the same as old energy clings to old. But those souls who are aware and use intent to take the truth will begin to move between these Earths freely. Unfortunately that point may be too late to get on the train and it is like missing the big Christmas party when the goodies are handed out. How this New Earth unfolds into view and how you deal with the Old Earth as it begins to fade out of view is an individual choice.

The key words of wisdom are this. Take your Train Ticket knowing in your heart there is a New Earth forming. On Old Earth remain in a space of non engagement and walk above that which you perceive as wrong or in judgement. Walk the Old Earth with a love for all and look upon all things with reverence as perfect the way they are, simply like you, in a state of evolving. Accept everything and resist nothing for that which you resist persists and energy flows where attention goes. You have a task at hand and need not engage in that which brings conflict, tears, pain or fear for they will eventually be known as only perceptions. Old Earth will begin to shift and will lose its hold upon you and soon as you see the shift of physicality you will resurrect yourself into your true self. Be patient with this and be steadfast, remember to love, laugh, live as one heart in every moment as your Train heads to Heaven.

But here is the truth of it. God will love you despite yourself because in the end, you already are He, regardless of what you may believe.

What is written on the ticket is simple:

By accepting this ticket you agree that you give pure intent to live as your true self in a world of unconditional love and accept your Divine gifts.

Then all you have to do is sit back and enjoy the ride.

There is one more question that you may want to ask. Is this new version of end Times credible in its source of information? First it is a fact that human consensus creates the human mass consciousness. Second, during the time of Revelation, millions of "psychic channels" have come forward with a new consensus of truth and it is escalating exponentially. Third, this is coming directly from the Co-creators from the guidance of Source.

So the real question comes back to you. Do you want to serve the gods or be God? It is time to Choose.

Choose well.

**For other titles by Ed Rychkun, go to
www.edrychkun.com**